FIRST PETER

A Translation and
Devotional Commentary

FIRST PETER

A Translation and Devotional Commentary

E. M. BLAIKLOCK

WORD BOOKS, PUBLISHER
WACO, TEXAS

FIRST PETER: A TRANSLATION AND DEVOTIONAL COMMENTARY

Copyright © 1977 by Word Incorporated, Waco, Texas 76703.
All rights reserved.
No part of this book may be reproduced in any form,
except for brief quotations in reviews,
without the written permission of the publisher.

Printed in the United States of America
ISBN 0-8499-0006-9
Library of Congress catalog card number: 77-075459

Unless otherwise noted, all quotations from Scripture and from classical
authors are the translation of the author. Other translations used are
listed on page 6.

Discipulis Meis
Bible College of N.Z.
MCMLXXV

The following translations of the Bible are referred to in the text:

KJV   —The King James or Authorized Version of the Bible

RSV   —The Revised Standard Version of the Bible, copyrighted 1946, 1952, © 1971, 1973 by the Division of Christian Education of the National Council of the Churches of Christ in the U.S.A., used by permission.

NAS   —The New American Standard Bible © the Lockman Foundation 1960, 1962, 1963, 1968, 1971

NEB   —*The New English Bible*, © The Delegates of The Oxford University Press and the Syndics of The Cambridge University Press 1961, 1970, used by permission.

NTBE   —*The New Testament in Basic English*, Cambridge University Press.

Goodspeed   —*The New Testament: An American Translation* by Edgar J. Goodspeed, copyright © 1923, 1948 by the University of Chicago.

Knox   —*The Holy Bible: A Translation from the Latin Vulgate in the Light of the Hebrew and Greek Originals*, by Msgr. Ronald Knox, © 1944, 1948, 1950 by Sheed and Ward.

LB   —*The Living Bible, Paraphrased*, copyright © 1971 by Tyndale House Publishers, used by permission.

Moffatt   —*The Bible: A New Translation*, by James Moffatt, copyright 1922, 1924, 1926, 1935, 1964 by James Moffatt, Harper & Row, Publishers.

Montgomery   —*The Centenary Translation: The New Testament in Modern English* by Helen Barlett Montgomery, copyright © 1924, 1952 by the American Baptist Board of Education and Publication, published by Judson Press.

Phillips   —*The New Testament in Modern English*, by J. B. Phillips, © 1958, 1960, 1970, by J. B. Phillips, published by Macmillan.

TCNT   —*The Twentieth Century New Testament*, Moody Press.

Weymouth   —*The New Testament in Modern Speech* by Richard Francis Weymouth, Harper & Row, Publishers.

Contents

Introduction

The Christians

The first letter of Peter, written in the early sixties of the first century to a great circle of churches in the rugged blunt peninsula which we call Asia Minor, is a document of immense historical and contemporary significance. A map will show how the peninsula of Asia Minor bridges the continents. We know a little, a very little, about how the Christian communities came to the administrative areas of the provinces of Asia and Galatia. We know something, and can guess a little more, of the activities of Paul, Barnabas, Silas, John and Timothy. We know nothing about how the Church came to Bithynia except from two notable letters of the governor of that province to Trajan early in the second century, by which time the area was heavily Christian. Of the Church in Pontus and in Cappadocia we know nothing.

9

But consider the notable fact. In a little over a generation after the death of Christ, communities of Christians were everywhere—up the river valleys which radiated from the Central Asian plateau, down to the ports of Ephesus and Smyrna, in the highlands round Antioch, Iconium, Lystra, and also in the rugged back areas toward the Black Sea. What drive and passion to evangelize lay behind this tremendous movement of missionary effort!

And also ponder this. Peter speaks to his Christian communities, as Paul also did, as aliens and strangers. They had broken with the Roman Empire and the empire was about to react to their challenge. It was a moment of crisis, for Rome and for the world. We catch the great political system at the moment of its choice. It is obvious that Paul had a vision—to establish the Church in the main centers, military, religious, cultural and political, of the great system which the genius of Augustus had pulled into unity when Christ was a boy at school in Nazareth. Had the empire accepted the faith, the Middle Ages might have been avoided. The rise of the army to political power might have been checked. Slavery, the social cancer in the world, would have slowly died. The frontiers would not have hardened, dividing the world into two camps. Evangelism would have crossed them and civilized outer Barbary. The Dark Centuries might never have fallen on the world. When in incredible folly the empire turned to suppression, it demonstrated its own mortal malady. Acceptance of a new form of life which had its origin in the body of Rome might have ensured a new burst of creative energy.

The future lay not with the imperial system, not with the legions from whose lawlessness the empire was to die. It lay with the Church, struggling to organize itself and destined to absorb, transmute and pass on all that was of lasting worth in the ancient world and the cultures which formed its seedbed. That is why this epistle is of such importance as a mere document of history. A man of faith and prescience can see the storm coming and therefore speaks to its certain victims on whose survival the future of the world depended. Never in the history of man had more been "owed by so many to so few."

The Romans

Rome seemed secure, her frontiers still assailed but largely as Augustus had defined them. They were to hold in comparative strength for another two centuries, and precariously for more than a century beyond that. At the same time, when military rebellion drove Nero to suicide in A.D. 68, a storm which almost shattered the empire was to break. A.D. 69 was the year of the four emperors, the time when "the Beast was wounded to death, recovered from her deadly wound" and made "all the world wonder after the Beast" (see Rev. 13). The frontier army corps learned what Tacitus, the great historian, called "the secret of Empire," that authority could be confronted and outfaced, and that a frontier army camp could make an emperor. That was the weakness from which the empire was to die.

The same decade saw the fearful revolt of the Jews and virtual destruction of Palestine. In grimmest truth the world ended for the Jews of the empire in the capture and the burning of Jerusalem. It was fear of the inevitable clash between the Jews and the Romans, a disaster which was in full view from the early sixties of the century, which put the note of warning and the certainty of trial and tribulation into Peter's message. He could not well foresee the catastrophe of the Great Fire and the events which followed. But equally, knowing the mood of the city and the wild doings of Nero, he could hardly escape the conclusion that there was trouble coming for his people—a trouble which, apart from the sinister hatred of the mob, the Christians could not well escape.

The end was truly near—the end of peace, the end of an era, of a chapter—but not of all things, at least for those who trusted Christ. For them death, as men knew and know it, was not the end. And in such a world as Christians inhabit today, can such a message lack relevance? The end could be near for any one of us, for any Church community, for tolerance, freedom, the very structure of human society. It is often later than we think.

In Keble College, Oxford, hangs the original of Holman Hunt's painting *Light of the World*. It is in the chapel, smaller than the copy in St. Paul's Cathedral, but showing a greater warmth of color and telling symbolism. It is clearly autumn. The Queen Anne's lace among the weeds which choke the door is heavy with its seed heads. Ripe apples lie on the ground. It is late in the year as well as late in the day. The shadows wait in the background ready to close in when the Figure in the foreground, on which all the illumination centers, departs with his light.

It is dangerous to by-pass history. Its patterns, man being still man, and God enduring, are strangely uniform. There is no doubt at all that this century is not a springtime of the world. Seeing the lamps in Westminster go out on the night of August 3, 1914, Sir Edward Grey said to a friend: "The lamps are going out all over Europe. We shall not see them lit again in our lifetime." For much of Europe that word was true. Much that shone in 1914 is gone from the world. There is a light, to be sure, which still shines in darkness, a darkness "which has not overtaken it" (John 1:5).

When John wrote those words he could look back on the night which fell on Peter's evening and thank God that it was true. Braced by such words as Peter wrote, the Christians outlived their foes. And for those who died, there broke the dawn for which they confidently hoped. " 'The dream is ended,' " said Aslan in C. S. Lewis's *The Last Battle*, " 'this is the morning.' " (New York: Macmillan, Collier Books, 1970, p. 183).

Is there ever a time, an age, a life for which such a message is without meaning? Dark shadows lie over the landscape of human life. Those who follow Christ still need the old courage, the old zeal, the old fortitude which can come only by the confidence that Christ is indeed the risen Savior, and by which they turn that faith to reality in the terms of daily life.

The Writer

If these introductory remarks are to bear the weight they claim, it must, admittedly, be established that the letter proceeds from its traditional source, the mind and authority of the apostle and leader of the Church, Simon Peter.

In common with that of every other document in the New Testament, the traditional authorship has, of course, been challenged, sometimes with subtlety, often perversely, seldom objectively, and nearly always on grounds which would not be regarded as valid by competent scholarship in any other sphere of historical and literary criticism.

To a professional classicist and historian, the world of biblical scholarship so often appears a somewhat alien environment, a closed world of cultivated skepticism, where tradition is automatically rejected, and where methods of investigation are habitually used which in classical studies would be set aside as naïve or irresponsible.

Consider two objections to the authenticity of the first letter of Peter. It is written in good, if sometimes slightly involved, Greek. It is not colored by the sometimes awkward Greek of the Septuagint, the Alexandrian translation of the Old Testament commonly in use in the bilingual world of the Early Church, in spite of the fact that quotations show that the writer was well acquainted with this widely used version.

Such competence in the Greek language, it is astonishingly claimed, could hardly have been achieved by a Galilean fisherman. In fact, the fisherfolk of Galilee were a prosperous and intelligent body of men, engaged in the busiest industry of the region. They were bilingual, living across the sea of Galilee from the Decapolis region, which had probably a million Greeks scattered through its towns and busy on the lake. Anyone who visits the Middle East today is aware of the ease with which ordinary people, including children, slip from language to language.

To be sure, a group of supercilious Sanhedrists,

preoccupied with Hebrew purism and contemptuous of Aramaic spoken with a broad Galilean accent, once described Peter, among others, as "illiterate" (Acts 4:13). This was about thirty years before the date here claimed for the letter. That any responsible literary critic could assert that here lay grounds for denying that Peter could have written such Greek as is found in his letter passes comprehension.

Any classically trained scholar today, brought up in the old tradition of Latin and Greek prose composition, can write sophisticated Greek and Latin in various styles, those perhaps of Caesar, Cicero, Demosthenes, Herodotus, Xenophon. It would not be too difficult for a good Hellenist to rewrite the first letter of John in the style of Peter, and for a good classicist to converse in Greek and Latin. I myself, as Public Orator of the University of Auckland, often framed for formal occasions addresses in Ciceronian Latin, for presentation to sister universities or learned societies. One sometimes wonders how linguistically aware some New Testament commentators are.

If wider illustration is sought, literature can provide many examples. Gibbon was equally fluent in French and English. Joseph Conrad (Josef Konrad Korzeniowski) was born of Ukrainian Polish parents in 1857, and spent 1874 to 1878 in the French mercantile marine. From 1878 to 1884 he climbed to master's rank in British merchant ships.

In 1894 at the age of 37, he deserted the sea to devote himself to English literature. His novels, from 1895 to 1920 (he died in 1924), are models of English prose.

Another objection to Petrine authorship, equally untenable, is the apparent "dependence" of the letter on "Paulinism." Paul's synthesis of the Testaments was, by the sixties, part of the doctrinal treasure of the Church. True, Peter had found it more difficult than Paul to extricate himself from Judaism. He had once clashed with Paul, but that was a score of years before. What is more likely than that someone writing from Rome should show an intimate knowledge of the letter to the Roman church, and that one writing to Ephesus in Asia, among other places, should show some acquaintance with the Ephesian epistle of Paul? Paul himself, in the early fifties, had been strong enough in his repudiation of fundamental differences between his own and Peter's gospel when that ugly form of sectarianism raised its head in the disorderly little Corinthian church.

Any perceptive reader of the letter will also be aware that the writer was a witness of Christ's ministry and passion. The sufferings and resurrection of Christ are woven with the text. The letter is haunted by the Sermon on the Mount. The writer had witnessed the transfiguration, the washing of the disciples' feet, had been called to feed the flock of God and had seen the risen Lord by the lake. He knew, as Paul did, of "the new birth," a story not to be linked with narrative until John wrote about Nicodemus three decades later.

Add finally the fact that, as far back as evidence goes, the letter was known and quoted by the Early Church. Any challenge to Petrine authorship came only with the appearance of nineteenth-century skepticism, when anything once believed was suspect and open for attack on no other grounds than that another age had held to it.

The Date

The position taken in this commentary is that the letter was written to Christians who were soon to suffer. The likeliest period, as was suggested above, is in the early sixties before the two critical events— the outbreak of Nero's savage persecution, and the year 66, a major black-letter day for Rome, when the fearful Revolt of the Jews broke upon the world and, apart from its own intrinsic horror, set the stage for the first episode of military intervention into the succession to the principate, that is, the reign of the emperors. This was the social or political malady which the great Augustus had foreseen and from which the empire was, in the end, to die. True, the Neronian massacre fell heavily on the city Christians, and Peter wrote to an Asian circuit, in the Christianizing of which he may have played a part. At some point, Nero's persecution, which at first was personal, canalized, and incidental, became a principle embedded in a statute. How and when this took place is not known, but any outbreak of evil in the capital was likely to be reflected in provincial policy.

Any observant and responsible observer in Rome must have been aware that the Christians were unpopular. The ghetto and the right wing of the synagogue did nothing to soften the hostility of the proletariat against the Christian minority. That situation is evident from the story in Acts 19 of the riot in Ephesus. At the same time, the same observer would undoubtedly know that the situation in the East was deteriorating. It required no gift of prophecy to see that open war was coming. It resembled the thirties of this unhappy century. Add the two menaces together and it may well be seen why the letter is full of warning and exhortation about impending disaster. There is no point in the first century which better reflects such a situation than the early sixties of that hundred years.

Whether the hand of the persecutor actually did fall with weight on the semicircle of churches in the peninsula of Asia Minor is not known. The period is not well documented, and it is only the fortunate survival of the two letters of Pliny to Trajan, written when Pliny governed the province of Bithynia in A.D. 111 and 112, which reveals how strong was the current of Christianity which was to flow, and must have been already flowing, round those regions.

The letter, then, can be taken up and read with confidence. It is authentic, it is true, it is real, it is somberly relevant to a modern world which has not done with evil, persecution and hostility to the Church. Nor, let us trust and back that trust with fearless action, has the same world seen the last of the power of Christ. "Be swift my soul to answer him, be jubilant my feet."

··{1}··

For Christians
in an Alien World

Peter, an apostle of Jesus Christ to the Chosen
who live abroad, scattered through Pontus, Galatia,
Cappadocia, Asia and Bithynia, those whom God the
Father knew and chose, through his Spirit's sanctify-
ing, that they should obey as befitted those sprinkled
by the blood of Jesus Christ—to you be grace and
peace, more and more (1:1–2).

It requires some effort of the mind to realize that
the writer of this authoritative preamble to a piece
of international correspondence was a man who,
some thirty years earlier, had made his living as a
fisherman in the narrow world of lakeside Galilee.
The hills of little farms and olive groves rose behind
the bays where the prosperous boatmen of the lake
plied their craft. The sun rose over the mauve wall
of the Golan Heights across the level silver of the
deep water—water which could be lashed to fury
when the north wind tore down the great Rift
Valley from the Beqaa between the Lebanon Ranges

and on to the Dead Sea down in the hot hollow of the wilderness.

It must have seemed very far away to Peter, and yet only yesterday, the day which took fisherfolk from Capernaum and Galilee down to the Jordan's mouth, seventy miles away, where the fiery John the Baptist was leading one of the greatest religious revivals the land had ever seen. And then, intimately tied to the forerunner's ministry, had come the three years with Jesus Christ. How perennially fresh in memory was that experience may be seen from this letter to the scattered Christians of Asia Minor.

A map will show the route taken by the messenger who carried the letter through a great circle of territory. He landed, perhaps at Sinope, on the Black Sea coast, and left by the port of Nicomedia. Much of this territory was outside the limits of the evangelism recorded in Acts. It runs in a more northerly arc. Paul was prevented from penetrating Bithynia (Acts 16:7). It is known, however, from the correspondence interchanged between the governor of the province and the Emperor Trajan (which survives as the Tenth Book of Pliny's letters), that in A.D. 110 or 111 the area was so solidly Christian that the temples were deserted, creating a problem for the trades whose subsistence was dependent upon pagan worship—the very situation of Acts 19. Vast tracts of Christian activity went unrecorded. We could wish that we knew more.

The theologically loaded language is common in the letters of the New Testament. The recipients had no corpus of Christian literature. They were instructed in set forms of words ("I received of the Lord that which I passed on to you . . ."), in theological hymns, and by the continued reiteration of Christian truth. Observe that Peter succeeds in packing into this introductory greeting, into verse 2 in fact, the functions of the Trinity and the end of salvation—committal to Christ.

The Christian congregations are described as "the Chosen," just as Israel had been a "Chosen People" (Deut. 4:37; Isa. 43:21; Rom. 11:28). The new Israel inherited the term. From the days of Abraham, Israel regarded itself as a race of strangers, sojourners, exiles (Gen. 23:4), looking for a habitation more real than any home or fatherland on earth (Heb. 11:10, 11; 13:14). Adolf Deismann, pioneer of papyrology, quotes the will of a Jew in the Fayum in Egypt, one Apollonion, who describes himself by Peter's very word—a sojourner, exile, foreigner, as distinct from a national. Is it not still true that the Christian commonly finds himself alien and remote from the "culture," the environment in which he lives? There is much in a pagan world which he cannot share.

"Dispersion" (rsv) was another term thus historically appropriated. Moses had foretold the uprooting and scattering of his people (Deut. 28:25),

and it is from the Septuagint translation of this verse
that *diaspora* (dispersion) entered the languages of
Europe. The Diaspora was to serve the gospel well.
The Greeks after Alexander had infiltrated the
eastern lands of the Mediterranean world. The Jews
had similarly moved westward. The fusion made the
New Testament and the Hellenistic Jews like
Philip, Stephen and Paul historically possible. A
great purpose flows through it all. The synagogues
made many Gentiles aware of God. They were
catalysts and stepping stones for the Gospel. The
first Christian cells often emerged from them.

> Praise be to the God and Father of our Lord Jesus
> Christ, who, by his great mercy, has given us new
> birth, into a living hope, through the resurrection of
> Jesus Christ from the dead, that we should be heirs
> to that which cannot perish, decay or fade away, and
> is stored for you in heaven . . . (1:3–4).

Exile was made endurable by hope, and hope—a
living, vital force—was based on a risen Christ.
Note that the death of Christ is immediately linked
with his resurrection (v. 3). The writer, it should
be remembered, was one of two who ran to the tomb
in the murk of the morning, and "saw the linen
clothes lying, and the cloth which had been about
his head . . . folded up by itself apart" (John
20:6–7). He spoke of no myth, no delusion, but of
an experience, which had transformed his life.

Hence the paean of praise to God which opens with verses 3 and 4 and runs on to verse 12.

Peter, like Paul, knows all about the doctrine of the "new birth," not to be explicitly developed until John told of the visit of Nicodemus, thirty years after Peter wrote these words. The newborn children of God have also, as children of a wealthy Father, an inheritance, not to be wildly spent (Luke 15:13, 14), or pilfered by theft—as open as burglary, or disguised as inflation—which like the eroding rust and the nibbling grub destroys the stored wealth of earth (Matt. 6:20). Peter is remembering the hillside looking north along the lakeshore to Tiberias, the Tabgha vale below, and the words of a sermon he could never forget.

Peter uses three adjectives all beginning with the same vowel, one of his small elegances of style, to describe the "inheritance." To object that a Galilean could not have achieved some polish in the writing of Greek is to misunderstand the linguistic patterns of the ancient world. From the days of Alexander, Greek had penetrated the Mediterranean world. It was the second tongue of the Middle East. Peter had lived in the presence of Greeks all his life and, for a generation, had lived in cities where Greek was the common language. Even in Rome it was used along with Latin. Not half a century later Juvenal, the Roman satirist, was complaining that Rome was becoming a Greek city, and worse, the East was pouring in and "the Orontes had become a tributary of the Tiber." It was pointed out in the introduction that Joseph Conrad, a Polish seaman, wrote glowing and powerful English though he knew nothing of the language until he was a grown man. Gibbon wrote French as readily as English.

Peter's first adjective, "imperishable" (KJV) or "incorruptible," is used four times by Paul (Rom. 1:23; 1 Cor. 9:25 and 15:52; 1 Tim. 1:17). This may have no significance, but it is clear from this letter that Peter knew Paul's letters well. "Inheritance" (KJV), as a figure of speech, is also Pauline, but goes back to earlier concepts. (Consider Matt. 25:34; Luke 10:25; 18:18; Rom. 4:13, 14; 8:17, 18; 1 Cor. 6:9, 10; 15:50; Gal. 5:21; Eph. 5:5.) The metaphor picks up the Old Testament thought of "inheriting" the land.

> . . . you who are guarded through faith by the power of God for the salvation ready to be revealed at the last time. Exult in it, though for a time, if need be, you have been made to sorrow in all manner of trials, so that the testing of your faith, which is something more precious than perishable gold—and even gold is tried by fire—may be found to win praise, glory and honor, when Jesus Christ appears (1:5–7).

Peter again almost echoes a phrase of Paul—Romans 1:16: "the power of God for salvation to everyone with faith." Those in Christ are "guarded," "garrisoned" by God along the infested and perilous path which leads to a goal and to a time (v. 5). Salvation in the New Testament is that wholeness which, like John's "eternal life," can be known, received and experienced in the present, but will find complete disclosure and realization in some day of consummation. Salvation is deliverance, and is it not part of common experience that deliverance from any danger, any oppression or servitude, cannot be fully enjoyed until some position of finality or completeness is reached? Meanwhile it is there, a present reality, a deep sustaining source of courage and of hope.

Hence the call to rejoicing in spite of the coming time of "testing" (v. 7). The word is that of the Beatitude (Matt. 5:11, 12). Grief, sorrow, it is recognized, inevitably come (John 16:20), for the circumstances of life bear hard upon the Christian's faith in multitudinous ways. Peter uses a vivid adjective. It is literally "many-colored trials," and in 4:10 he uses the same word to describe the grace of God.

Christians can endure, Peter says, for two strong reasons. First, let them look on trouble as a testing of faith, a fire which burns out the impurities and leaves faith purer and stronger. As such it is a precious thing. Peter thus echoes Romans 5:3, 4. The second reason for endurance is the Coming Day. It was mentioned at the end of verse 5. It is further defined at the end of verse 7. The Lord himself will be revealed along with the deliverance he gave. Men can endure much when "praise, glory and honor" not of this world's bestowing but a gift incorruptible and uncorrupting, borne on the words of Christ—the ultimate "well done"—is visible beyond the darkened horizons of pain. "A star will glow like a note God strikes on a silver bell," gasps the old knight in Masefield's poem "The Ballad of Sir Bors," stumbling on in quest of the Grail, "And the sight of the Rose, the Rose, will pay for the years of Hell . . ." It is no Grail the Christian seeks but the ultimate joy when "we shall be like him; for we shall see him as he is" (1 John 3:2, KJV).

> Whom, though you have not seen him, you love, whom, though you do not now see him, yet believing in him, you rejoice with joy unspeakable and full of glory, receiving the goal of your faith, your souls' salvation (1:8–9).

In reading this lyrical passage, remember again the man who wrote it, and of whom he wrote. Peter walked with Christ, and one of the marks of the Lord's unearthly personality is to observe its impact upon the lives of those whom he had once called to follow him and be "fishers of men." In most human fellowship, familiarity brings a measure of disillusionment. Our friends, however enthusiastic the

beginning of friendship may be, soon reveal themselves as we are, human and faulty. A friendship
survives on these terms. Forgiving, now whimsi-
cally, sometimes with humor, sometimes with a
whiff of impatience, we give and take in mutual
indulgence. Not so with Christ and his men. They
trod together the roads of Galilee and Judea. They
sailed the lake, slept under the stars, ate together by
the well and on the beach, pressed through the
crowds, confronted the pompous and the poor,
shared a life of uncommon intimacy and difficulty.
From Bethany to Tyre they lived with him.

Far from detecting the hidden flaws of common
character, the bad temper fired by tension, loosed by
weariness; far from becoming aware of the ulterior
motive, the concealed ambition, so often damagingly
betrayed in human conversation by the hasty word,
the unwise slip; far indeed from discovering at all
the blemishes of the flesh, they felt awe and reverence grow. The fact may be observed in this same
Peter, who is the most sharply portrayed in the narrative of all the Twelve. He was a man always ready
to talk and to put his first reactions into words. He
earned, indeed, rebuke (Matt. 16:22–24). But he
grows silent as the road ends. At the supper, after
the one quick and gloriously transformed remark
when Christ washed his feet, Peter at the table can
only beckon to a younger friend to whisper and ask
who the traitor might be (John 13). Later, as he

stands in agony by the brazier in the courtyard, one glance from his Master breaks him (Luke 22:61–62).

And now see what he writes of the Man he knew. The same astonishing phenomenon is to be found in John's writings—in the Gospel, in his letters, in the visions of the Apocalypse. James called his brother "the Lord of Glory." Could there be a stranger proof of some transforming and utterly wondrous event? And what else but the Resurrection? Link verse 8 with John 20:29. Peter heard those words and they never left him. In Greek, as in the English of the KJV, the verse is rhythmic language.

But now observe. The pronoun is "you," not "we." These early Christians, addressed thus in their towns and villages across Asia Minor, had, as Peter says, never seen Christ, and yet they responded in these terms of loyalty and love. In them we meet the confidence and certainty of the first witnesses to the living Christ, as it emerged in the faith and joy of those who had simply heard them or their more immediate converts. We are moving outward from the first volcanic outburst of the faith and discovering the same ardor of conviction which shook Jerusalem at Pentecost. Its transmission is remarkable.

In the translation the word "glory" of the KJV has been retained. Literally the text runs: ". . . with joy unspeakable and glorified." The word *glory* is a trifle archaic. Thomas Hobbes in his

Leviathan, written over three centuries ago, defined laughter acutely as "sudden glory." He meant that laughter is best explained psychologically as an expression of an exalted mood of gladness, that stirring of the heart at something won, achieved, wondrously given. This draws near to the mood of triumphant fulfillment of the human spirit filled with confidence in Christ.

The word translated "receiving" is an interesting one. It is found in the Classical Greek orators in the sense of "recovering" a debt, the use in Matthew 25:27: "I should have recovered my investment with interest." Paul is fond of the word (2 Cor. 5: 10; Eph. 6:8; Col. 3:25; and see also Heb. 11:39). In the final word of verse 9 Peter returns to the consummation of the believer's faith, the fulfilled and perfected "salvation." It is what was promised, the sure prize to which they moved, a prize most certainly to be delivered.

Yes, a salvation into the nature of which the prophets, who by inspiration spoke of the grace which should come to you, made most diligent inquiry, seeking to discover the occasion and the nature of the occasion which the Spirit of Christ within them was indicating, when it bore witness beforehand to the sufferings of Christ and the splendors to follow them. To them it was revealed that not for themselves but for us they were exercising this ministry—a message now made clear to you by those who brought you the gospel with the help of the Holy Spirit sent from heaven, truths into which angels long to look (1:10–12).

This is a packed and crowded passage, as though the eager writer sought to use every inch of papyrus and every moment of time, to pack the truths of two Testaments into one paragraph. Peter is catching up a saying of Christ's (Matt. 13:17; Luke 10:24), in which the wonders of the day of God's visitation were stressed. He shared with the writer of the letter to the Hebrews (11:13–16) the conviction that the Old Testament prophets were aware, or became aware, that the words they felt impelled to preach in the context of their own day and situation were loaded with a deeper meaning. He has in mind such passages as Psalm 22, Isaiah 52:13–53:12 and Psalms 2 and 16.

God's grace and salvation's plan are taken too easily for granted. It was Socrates who said that he supposed that God, being omnipotent, was able to do anything, but that he could not see how, being holy, he could forgive sin. Hence the atonement. He was able to be just, and at the same time forgive (1 John 1:9), because of the Cross. Anything, therefore, which demeans the atonement also diminishes God.

Grace is a wondrous thing, and Peter showed his sensitive appreciation of its wonder when he imagined the prophets amazed at implications in their own words, and angels astonished at what the mind of God had devised for man's salvation. "I wish to hear of Thulcandra [earth] and of Maleldil's strange wars there with the Bent One," says the ruler of Malacandra (Mars) in C. S. Lewis's fantasy *Out of the Silent Planet.* "Tell me all" (New York: Macmillan, 1955, pp. 132, 133).

Curiously, the verb used for the angels' looking into the wonder of the Plan is the very word used for John bending down to peer into the sepulchre in the murk of the morning, after he had outdistanced Peter in the run to the tomb in the garden. Is it possible that the image of peering in was still present to Peter's mind, tangled with that undying memory? And is he continuing the chain of recollection of the forty days in the next verse? But first let us translate. . . .

Therefore, girding up the loins of your minds, be self-controlled, and fix your hopes completely on the grace that is being brought to you with the Appearing of Jesus Christ . . . (1:13).

The long garments of the East impeded the free movement of the legs and were tucked up beneath a wide waistband or girdle for any vigorous action. Peter was lightly clad in his undergarment (this is what "naked" can mean, John 21:7, KJV) on that other dawn when they dimly saw a figure by a fire on the Galilee shore. He picked up his cloak, girded it at the middle, and splashed ashore. Hence the figure here. "Stripped for action," says the NEB; "brace up your minds," say Montgomery and Moffatt. There is a task to be done and a journey to be undertaken (Exod. 12:11 and Prov. 31:17).

Observe that the mind of the Christian is to be concentrated, stiffened, freed from impediment. Attempts to dissociate heart and mind in the experience and testimony of the Christian are as futile as they are foolish. We are given minds to use and apply, and the current exaltation, in some quarters, of "experience" and emotion is only occult sloth, an avoidance of hard thinking.

"Be self-controlled," Peter continues. "Sober" (KJV) is not a good word. It is specialized in modern English in two directions. It can mean "free from alcoholic intoxication." It can mean "glum and straight-faced," the vice alleged against the Puritan. But when a word is thus colored or tarnished, it is well to avoid it. The self-discipline of faith is what Peter has in mind. The steady mind, which never loses sight of purpose, goal and essentials, is the ideal—a mind alert to know the contents of faith, the task appointed, and able to recognize the circumstances, temptations and weaknesses, which can cling about the legs like entangling garments.

And the steadying thought is hope. There is an adverb in the verse which fundamentally means "perfectly." The NEB takes it with "self-con-

trolled," rendering it "perfectly" quite simply. The
KJV takes it with the command to hope—"hope to
the end." Montgomery agrees—"fix your hope
firmly." This is probably the better choice and is so
translated above. Barclay is too heavy—"Come to a
final decision to place your hope. . . ." He probably gives too much weight to the aorist imperative,
which strictly, of course, does denote a single act.
One might expect a present imperative here, the
"linear" command which would mean "go on hop-
ing," but, good though Peter's Greek is, the nicer
points of Classical grammar cannot be pushed too
closely in the Common or Koine Greek. To say that
the aorist imperative enjoins "a single act" does not,
in any case, limit that act to an instant in time. The
immediate command can view the rest of life as one
movement of hope, and let that hope be exercised
"perfectly," that is without wavering or fear. The
hope lies in the consummation of that which grace
has begun.

> . . . like obedient children, not trying to adapt to
> the desires of your past ignorance, but just as the
> One who called you is holy, do you too prove your-
> selves godly people, in all the manner of your life—
> just as it stands written: "You shall be holy because
> I am holy" (1:14–16).

There is, as we have said, much evidence in this
letter that Peter knew what Paul had written to the

Roman church, especially chapter 12 of Romans. The word translated "fashioning yourselves" (KJV) is that used in Romans 12:2 for conforming oneself to the world—in other words allowing a base society, or in Peter's context a vicious stratum of the personality, to determine conduct. "Don't keep on trying to make yourself like the society you live in," says Paul; and Peter says "not continually adapting yourselves to the desires you had when you knew no better." It is God's indwelling Spirit, permeating the personality, governing the will, and so determining conduct and ultimately character, which should shape us. Obedience is the prerequisite.

Verse 15 presents the positive side of the exhortation: "but rather after the pattern of the Holy One who has called you, be godly in every department of your lives." For the ancient injunction see Leviticus 11:45 and Isaiah 52:11. The word *holy* is another word which has been damaged by human misuse and tainted by satire, such as Burns's "Holy Willie's Prayer," but it remains a Christian ideal. Its basic meaning is "kept apart for God's use" both in English and in Greek, and so the Christian must in humility regard himself.

The life of the pagan, then as now, was one of ignorance, for what ignorance is as deep and damaging as that which cannot recognize life's purpose and goal? It is a life governed by base desires, for there is in it no governance of an informed and enlightened mind over the animal self and the desires of the body. The literature of the first century provides illustration enough, exiguous though its remains are, to justify the strictures of Paul at the beginning of the Roman letter. Peter's people followed a holy God. They could do no other but obey him. "Children of obedience," which is what the Greek says literally, is a Hebraism for "obedient children" (see Col. 3:6 and Eph. 2:2; 5:6). In the Beatitude, "children of God" means similarly "Godlike" (Matt. 5:9).

"Show yourselves in the whole pattern of your lives," is another way of translating the end of verse 15. The word Peter uses for manner of life is what the KJV frequently terms one's "walk." In its verbal form it appears in the Septuagint in Proverbs 20:7: "the good man walks righteously." (Peter uses it again in the next verse, and in 2:12 and 3:1 he has the corresponding noun). One's manner of walking always reveals something of the personality —purposeful, vigorous, slouching, arrogant, aimless. And we are, he says, to "become" holy. The thought behind the word is probably "become what you were not in your earlier mode of living," or "show yourselves," "emerge visibly," obvious to the onlooking world as someone different. In any case the notion of becoming is encouraging. It implies no sudden sinless perfection, an impossible injunction. It rather bids us seek what is in reach of every one of us, a progress to a goal, a "wrestle on towards heaven," as John Greenleaf Whittier's hymn puts it.

If you call Him Father, who judges everyone with complete impartiality, according to what he does, live out the time of your sojourn with reverence, knowing that you were not ransomed with perishable things such as silver and gold from the captivity of the aimless life you had inherited, but by the precious blood of Christ, as a lamb umblemished and spotless—Christ, foreknown indeed from the world's beginning, but for you made known in these last days—you who through him believe in God who raised him from the dead, and gave him glory, so that your faith and hope should be fixed on God (1:16–21).

An alternate rendering of verse 16: "If you address him as Father who without favoritism judges us by what we do, reverence must be the keynote of your lives." Christ called God *Father*, and bequeathed the term to us. Peter is echoing the Lord's Prayer, another vivid reminiscence and an indication that the Prayer was already in wide use (Jer. 3:19; Ps. 84:26). God is not simply the "ultimate reality," an intangible "ground of our being." He may be both, but only if he is also near, real, comprehensible, loving as a father, gentle as a shepherd, generous as a host. For so he redeemed us from "futile living" (v. 18), the barren pattern into which Judaism had slipped, a bondage hard to break, so hard that it claimed Christ's life and death to shatter it (v. 19). That ultimate revelation was, says Peter, their privilege. It is also ours to tell in the language of today, but never to lose, spoil or diminish.

A few interesting words should be examined. Note the word rendered "with complete impartiality," "without the slightest favoritism" (Phillips), "without respect of persons" (KJV). The metaphor embedded in the word (an adverb here, an abstract noun at Rom. 2:10) means literally "not receiving the face of someone." It is the metaphor of 1 Samuel 16:7: "Look not on his countenance, . . . " echoed by Paul (2 Cor. 10:7). The face can deceive and hide "the thoughts and intents of the heart" (Heb. 4:12, KJV). It can be a mask. In the Greek word used in Peter's adverb, and in Paul's half quotation of the phrase from 1 Samuel 16:7, the Greek word *prosōpon* appears, which can actually mean the mask always worn by the actors in Greek tragedy and comedy. God is not deceived by "made-up" faces or by masks of any sort. He sees the core of the personality (1 Kings 8:39). But note especially that Peter is again back in the notable days of the first events of his ministry. "In truth I understand," he said to the centurion of Caesarea, "that God is no receiver of faces," "respecter of persons" (Acts 10:34). He is using the word of verse 17 as a noun.

Already in this chapter we have noted several references to vividly remembered events of Peter's past. One critic of seventy years ago (Von Soden, quoted in *The Expositor's Greek New Testament*, vol. 4 [Grand Rapids, Mich.: Eerdmans, 1952], fn., p. 11) wrote: "It is evident that St. Peter cannot have written this epistle . . . how, especially at such a time, could he have refrained from speaking of reminiscences which formed the best, the most inspiring, message that he could deliver?" Here is illustration of my introductory remark—it seems doubtful sometimes whether those who profess to expound New Testament criticism can read Greek with ease. We have already seen such references, and we shall see more. Anyone who approaches the New Testament after the more rigorous discipline of classical Greek and Latin is continually amazed at the uninformed and sometimes quite irresponsible attitudes manifested in New Testament studies. Facts are too often ignored to safeguard a theory.

Pass on to the word "fear" (KJV) in the same verse. The word is used in two senses in the New Testament. To run through the references in any concordance will demonstrate the two classes. There is the fear which paralyzes and which love "casts out" (1 John 4:18, KJV), an unworthy fault, natural to the flesh and the imperfect heart of man, but to be resisted and bravely quenched. There is also

the salutary fear—of evil (Luke 12:5), of God
(2 Cor. 5:11), of failure (Phil. 2:12). This fear is,
rather, reverence. "Work out your own salvation,"
says Paul, "carry your salvation into effect, with
reverence and self-distrust" (Phil. 2:12). The
Latin word *reverentia* means "due" or "proper"
fear, and there is no sin in the recognition of the danger which besets all uprightness and the ambush
which awaits the good man's passing. There is
safety in reverence.

There is yet another word in this linguistically
rich verse which calls for brief notice. Peter speaks
of life as "the time of your sojourn." It is the abstract of the noun used in the address of the letter
(1:1), "strangers" (KJV), "sojourners." The
Christian's citizenship is in heaven. We are to live
worthily, says Paul, as citizens of our earthly community, but not to forget that we really belong to
another realm (Phil. 1:27; 3:20) and cannot feel
quite at home here. The word echoes the thought
of Ephesians 2:19, another letter which Peter must
have known.

They were "ransomed," says verse 18, without
money—an echo of Isaiah 52:3. It is a common
metaphor in both Testaments (Isa. 44:22–24;
Luke 24:21). Tradition was a harsh jailer, and they
had been held, in a manner both Peter and Paul
knew (Gal. 2:13, 14), by the bondage of all the
past. It was a powerful force to break, and could

have been broken only by a firm faith that in the Lamb without spot or blemish all the traditions of the past had been so effectively consummated that it was not only futile but sinful to cling to the shadow and lose the reality. In Christ was a finality envisaged by God long before its symbols were invented (v. 20), or its earthly preparation begun, and wondrously revealed to one fortunate and blessed generation. It is the theme of Colossians 2, a chapter which should be read. This letter of Peter may have indeed reached the Lycus valley where Colossae stood within walking distance of the towns of Laodicea and Hierapolis.

> Having purified your souls by your obedience to the truth, a process which issues in an undissembling love for one another, then show your love constantly, reborn as you are not of mortal but of immortal seed, through the living and lasting Word of God. For "all flesh is like grass, and its glory like the flower of grass. The grass withers and the flower fades, but the Lord's Word lasts for ever." And the gospel which was brought to you is that Word (1:22–25).

Peter anticipates the theme of John's first letter, the demonstration of Christian love. In that divided, stratified society it was very necessary. After all, born again, as the whole Christian body was, all distinction had been obliterated in a new and common parenthood. But just as the Jews found it difficult to claim and exercise their emancipation from tradition, so master and slave, aristocrat and commoner, found some lifelong habits of conduct hard to eradicate. James (2:1–3) touches on the problems, basing his argument on the fact that God is no respecter of persons (Peter's and Paul's word again), so what right have we to be?

Christianity, in fact, was penetrating all ranks of society. The word of Gibbon that the new sect was "almost entirely composed of the dregs of the populace—of peasants and mechanics, of boys and women, of beggars and slaves" is untrue. Apart from the amazing content, on the great historian's definition, of "the dregs of the populace," the assertion is without any foundation. True, there was a Christian cell in "Caesar's household" (Phil. 4:22), by which is meant the imperial civil service; there were no doubt slaves, but literary evidence suggests that the highest in the land were Christians, and before the death of the last apostle, the faith had a place in the emperor's family (see the writer's *Archaeology of the New Testament*, pp. 156–65).

That is by the way. Here we are imagining the problems of fellowship and adjustment between people drawn into one community by their faith. Hence the insistence of Peter and John on brotherly love. They were, after all, the only coherent group destined to survive the coming centuries. Hence the telling quotation from the most poetic of the prophets. Man is transient, his life like the fragile flower, frail as the feeble grass. God's Word, his eternal principles, endure.

The figure and image come from Isaiah 40:6–8, and for those who knew the Old Testament, the quotation would evoke the whole warm passage: "Comfort ye, comfort ye my people, saith the Lord, speak ye comfortably to Jerusalem . . ." (KJV). Read the first eleven verses of the passage and envisage it in the context of a menaced and harassed Christian minority, abashed and daunted by the might of Rome, hanging over them like a leaden sky. All the empire's glory was as the flower of the field. And so it proved. It was the Christian Church which absorbed, transmuted and passed on whatever was of lasting worth in the civilizations that contributed to its preparation and formed a seedbed for its first growth. When, in incredible folly, the empire turned to persecution, it demonstrated its own mortal malady. Acceptance of the new form of life which had found its origin in the body of Rome would have ensured a new burst of creative energy and the withering at the root of the cancers of slavery and armed insurrection by a corrupt and misled military force, from both of which the empire was to die. The Church lived, as it will always live, if the abiding Word is kept intact within her. Lose this, and all is lost.

··{2}··

For Christians
in a Pagan Society

So, putting off all malice, deceit, insincerity, jealousies and recriminations of every kind, like newborn babes long for the unadulterated milk of the Word, so that you may grow up by it into fullness of life—if indeed you have tasted that the Lord is gracious (2:1–3).

To understand any communication in literature, be it prose or poetry, there must be some attempt to conform to the mind of the author. Those who set out to read what another writes, in search of information, edification or inspiration, must come to the text in a spirit of surrender and acceptance. Hence the first verse. All tolerated "malice, deceit, insincerity, jealousies and recriminations of every kind," must be rooted from the recesses of the mind, if the reader of Scripture is to find the "sincere milk of the word" (KJV). The faith and alertness of the innocent child is a proper preparation for Bible study.

Peter names here many of the hindrances of life in any community. The clashes of personality which arise even among Christians are a hindrance to fellowship and true growth in grace. Observe the common element in all these social vices—the exaltation of self, thrusting another down that self may stand spuriously higher, the suicidal bitterness which issues in envy, and slander. These are heathen things which, like soiled garments, must be stripped off (v. 1). All these base faults issue in speech—the "talking down" disparagement of the last word in the list. And all inhibit what should be a deep desire (v. 2) for the nourishing food of God's Word. The apostles were tireless in their insistence that Christ in the life must change the conduct, dominate thought, tame the tongue. So was the Lord. The true Israelite, unlike their patriarch Jacob, was without deceit (John 1:47).

The second verse might be rendered: "Since you are but newborn babes, desire strongly. . . ." It is a continuation of the metaphor of 1:23. The verb is a strong one with a reinforcing prefix. Some translate the adjective *logikos* which we have rendered "of the Word," as "spiritual." In Romans 12:1 it occurs with the meaning "reasonable" ("the only service you can properly render"). As babes they must grow. Nothing is more pathetic than a child who never grows; and the object of the growth is that spiritual adulthood, maturity, completeness

which is rendered "salvation." "Grow into salvation" means simply that; or as the NEB renders:
"that you may thrive on it to your soul's health"—
a good translation, provided the idea of growing up
is contained in the phrase.

To sum up the passage: the words of Scripture
are the food on which the newborn spirit thrives. It
is obvious why this is so. The growth of the spirit is
growth in the understanding of God, in the knowledge of his will, and in the experience of his grace.
Once that blessedness has been in truth revealed to
an enlightened understanding (v. 3), a thirst and
hunger is born for more. Perhaps it is true to say
that such desire is the only sure sign of the soul's
salvation. Certain it is that there is no growth without it. Just as the physical body weakens and dies
without its proper sustenance, so the spirit sickens
and perishes without that which feeds it. As the
Beatitude has it, those who thirst are filled. There
is no promise, and no fulfillment, for those who lack
the desire. But for those who have tasted the goodness of God there can be no quenching of the desire
(Ps. 34:8).

> Approach him, a living stone, rejected indeed by
> men, but chosen and valued by God. And you also,
> as living stones, keep on building yourselves into a
> spiritual edifice, in which a sanctified priesthood may
> offer up spiritual sacrifices acceptable to God in Jesus
> Christ—for in Scripture it says: Look, I lay in Zion

a chosen Cornerstone, a precious one, and he who believes in him shall not be put to shame (2:4–6).

This is one of many passages of Scripture which can only be made plain by what Peter, and most of those to whom he wrote, had—an intimate knowledge of the Old Testament. The imagery and words of the Hebrew Scriptures formed a framework for their thought, and supplied prefabricated material for their speech and thinking. To us, without such background, the train of thought and the association of ideas may appear remote, tortuous, alien. But it was not so for the Jew, or for those who had found a home in the synagogue.

Verses 4, 5 and 6 are a cluster of such images. And it must be remembered that ancient writers cared nothing for the refinement of style which avoids mixed metaphor. It is possible to follow Peter's thought as his mind, soaked in the story of his people, leaps to picture after picture—first the rock from which the sustaining water sprang, then the cornerstone, rejected by the builders, and between both figures of speech there intrudes Paul's metaphor of the building of which each believer is a part, and whose whole structure is bound by the keystone of their Redeemer (see Exod. 17:6; Ps. 118:22; Isa. 8:14, 15 and 28:16; Matt. 21:42; Rom. 9:33; Eph. 2:15, 20).

Note, however, the important conclusion for the matter. Stones are of little use save that together,

properly knit and firmly placed, they can form a
useful edifice. Peter pictures the building as a tem-
ple with Christ holding the whole structure together. Then, with a rapid turn of thought, he sees
the body of Christians as a priesthood. And why not,
if a priest, in both the Jewish and pagan conception,
was a man with access to God? The Romans had a
word for priest which could possibly embody this
idea. *Pontifex* (Latin *pons* and *facio* are the roots)
meant a "bridge-maker," that is one who bridged
the gulf between man and God by formula, ritual or
sacrifice. The Christian has no need for such media-
tion. It was made by the one High Priest, as the
eloquent writer to the Hebrews knew (10:18–22).

> The worth of which I speak is for you who believe.
> For those who do not believe, the stone which the
> builders rejected and which became the Cornerstone,
> that same stone became a stone to stumble over, a
> stone to fall over—those, I mean, who stumble over
> the Word in their disobedience, which was their fate.
> But you are a chosen race, a royal priesthood, a dedi-
> cated nation, God's own people, that you might tell
> out the worth of him who called you out of darkness
> into his wondrous light—you who were once "no
> people," but now are God's people, who once knew
> no mercy, but now have found mercy (2:7–10).

The translation has been filled out a little to ease
the reader through the crowded words—words, of
course, familiar enough to those whose minds

worked within the patterns of Old Testament language.

To follow Peter's tumult of imagery, the reader must again bear in mind that the writer's education had been in the text and meaning of the Old Testament. Peter lacks Paul's complete familiarity with Greek culture. He lifts bodily from the ancient Hebrew Scriptures words and sayings which he conflates and links in new patterns to apply them to the New Testament Church.

The image of the stone is continued in verses 7 and 8 with a bold conjunction of Psalm 118:22 and Isaiah 8:14. The very stone which the builders rejected (RSV) has become a stone to trip over, and a rock to stumble at (Weymouth). The thought is that of 1 Corinthians 1:23–24: "We preach Christ crucified, to Jews a stumblingblock . . . but to those who are the called . . . Christ the power of God . . . " (NAS). Rejected truth is obviously dangerous. The sun which softens wax hardens the concrete—a thought first expressed by Origen, but an analogy which falls short of the truth, for it is deliberate and self-willed rejection which Peter has in mind, not an inflexible predestination. Phillips's translation brings out this thought in verse 8: "Yes, they stumble at the Word of God for in their hearts they are unwilling to obey it—which makes stumbling a foregone conclusion." God's word saves or condemns.

In the next verse Peter passes to another cluster of Old Testament word pictures. He conflates Isaiah 43:20–21 with Exodus 19:5, 6 and Psalm 107:14. The Church, the new Israel, has all the privileges of the Chosen People, indeed naturally inherits them. In Peter's tissue of transformed quotations may be seen the phenomenon to be observed in the hymns of the Nativity in the opening chapters of Luke's Gospel. Minds fed and filled with the language of Scripture resort instinctively to that medium for the tools of expression.

Verse 10 is a recollection in similar vein of Hosea 1:6–10. The lesson for the modern reader of the Bible is the possibility of so forming and shaping thought and outlook by the Word of God, by study and memorizing, that life's varied situations are met by its wisdom, just as the Lord in his temptation countered the words of Satan with nothing more than the text of Scripture. It is there that the Bible becomes "a lamp to the feet and a light to the path."

Before leaving this crowded passage consider the implication of the last two verses. The Christians of this world, a royal priesthood, a nation sanctified, a chosen people, are left among men to fulfill a vital function. The privilege is too casually accepted. The Christians alone have reality. From being of no standing, no worth, "the Remnant" of other Scripture images have become real, coherent, clean. It is a calling high enough to daunt and challenge. If man survives this menaced century it will be by means of a vast, cleansing return to God, and through whom can such a spiritual force find entrance into the crawling ruin of a pagan world save through the Christian Church? Never, indeed, as Churchill put it, in the whole field of human endeavour, "was so much owed by so many to so few."

Beloved, as aliens and exiles here, please keep yourselves away from the carnal passions which campaign against the soul, making your manner of living a fine one in a pagan world, so that, in the very sphere in which they slander you as doers of evil, observing your fine conduct, they may honor God when the time comes (2:11–12).

There is evidence everywhere in this epistle of the influence Paul's writings had on Peter. It is to be expected, in such a person as Peter, that practical chapters like Romans 12 would make a deep impression on him. Not that the opening words of this section, "Beloved, I beseech you, . . ." (RSV) need be an echo of Paul's appeal. Since *parakalo*, "I beseech," means "please" in modern Greek, I have ventured to assume that it was acquiring that meaning in the first century. "Aliens and exiles" is an echo of 1 Peter 1:1 and 17.

To "abstain from" (KJV) is literally "keep yourselves away from," and it is possible that a phrase of Plato, in his noblest dialogue, may have had general currency. True philosophers, he said, "keep themselves away from all carnal passions" (*Phaedo* 82:C). For Paul's parallel thought see Galatians 5:19–21 and Ephesians 2:3. "The flesh," of course, in New Testament thought, is something wider than the body. Paul's list includes sins of the mind or spirit. The notion of "the flesh" contains all the false and evil attitudes of a life outside of Christ, without Christ's norms and standards. The insistence of the apostles on the ethical requirements of Christian living is striking.

The Christian community had already opted out of the culture, if that overworked word may be used, in which their lot was cast. They had become citizens of another realm, as Paul told the Philippians, and so lived in this world like resident aliens. Like all minorities, they lived under scrutiny. Like all challenging minorities, they lived under critical and even hostile inspection. They were slandered. Their conduct was vilified, misrepresented and misunderstood. In this very area, Peter said, they must provide the refutation. The first front with the world was their uprightness of conduct. As Paul, already quoted, said, they must cease from all attempts to conform to the world's base standards, and by nobility of life, face an evil society by their manifest goodness. The same words apply today. It is not the Church which must adapt to the patterns of society, but the precise opposite. The Church must provide, and in the person of each Christian provide, a pattern which is impeccable, a goodness so manifest that the voice of a hostile world is silenced.

The Christians were, in fact, bitterly misrepresented. Tacitus, writing about A.D. 115, speaks of Nero's persecution of the Roman Christian community after the Great Fire of the summer of A.D. 64, within a year or two of the writing of this letter. Nero, probably with truth, was suspected of starting the enormous conflagration to clear away slums from the area of his great building schemes. The truth will never be known. Nero, lyre changed to fiddle, has come down the centuries in a proverb. But if those heavy features hid the secret of Rome's fire, the secret perished with the criminal five years later, and his accomplices held their peace. It is a fact, nonetheless, that Nero was terrified. The "many-headed beast," the proletariat of Rome, could be dangerous. Nero met the menace with a parade of religion, the consultation of oracles, public prayer and sacrifice. But popular emotion refused to be appeased. Some impressive demonstration seemed necessary, and at this point some villain with the emperor's ear conceived a dastardly idea. Tacitus writes:

"Neither human aid, nor imperial bounty, nor atoning offerings to the gods, could remove the sinister suspicion that the fire had been brought about by Nero's order. To put an end therefore to this rumor, he shifted the charge on to others, and inflicted the most cruel tortures upon a body of men detested for their abominations, and popularly known by the name of Christians. This name came from one Christus, who was put to death in the reign of Tiberius by the Procurator Pontius Pilatus; but though checked for the time, the detestable superstition broke out again, not in Judaea only, where the mischief began, but even in Rome, where every horrible and shameful iniquity, from every quarter of the world, pours in and finds a welcome."

Such is the shadow under which the Christians enter secular history. A year or two before, while Tacitus was governor of Asia, his friend Pliny, governor of the neighboring province of Bithynia, had written to the Emperor Trajan asking for a guideline in dealing with the Christians in his area. He spoke of the rumors about them, but adds that his secret agents had been able to discover nothing more reprehensible than "depraved superstition." Half a century after the great disaster in Rome, Tacitus's sources retained the old evil story at which Peter hints.

It was an expression of mass psychology. An uncompromising conscience had withdrawn the followers of Christ from participation in many of the activities of a society which was much more communal and closely knit than that of the Anglo-

Saxon world of today. The crowd has marked the abstinence, reacted as crowds react, and branded the abstainers with its disapproval. Crowds are feeble in reasoning and passionate in imagination. Hence, too often, the sad fate of minorities. Nero, like a hundred demagogues before and after him, seized on the ill-considered emotions of the mass, and exploited them. So, five years before, in a revealing incident, had the silversmiths of Ephesus (Acts 19). There was fuel for Nero's firing in the dislike which the compliant and conforming majority feel for the dissident and nonconforming few. The spectacle of moral earnestness, such is human nature, offends the morally inert, and the sight of disciplined living rebukes and angers self-indulgence. The vested interests of vice fear virtue, and corruption is uneasy in the presence of a sterner and challenging uprightness. So, in varied fashion, had Christians stirred the emotional hostility of the ancient crowd. Nero canalized the crowd's passion, gave it self-expression, and supplied a cover of logic for baseness, and a cloak of social righteousness for unreasoning hatred.

Such was the attitude, such were the execrable slanders, which Peter bids his people rebuff with upright living. The same command still holds.

For the Lord's sake submit to man's established authority, to the emperor as the supreme ruler, to the magistrates, commissioned by him for the judgment of criminals and to commend those who behave well—for this is God's will that by good behavior you may put to silence the ignorance of foolish people—as free men, but not using your freedom as a cover for misconduct, but as servants of God (2:13-16).

The great clash between Rome and the Church had not yet come, dark though its portents were on the horizon. Peter, like Paul, was urgent to impress upon the Christian groups that much depended upon their reputation as good citizens. It was not until the fear and sadism of Nero in A.D. 64 began the persecution of the Church, and the folly of the repressive legislation which followed it, that the Christians saw the State as a foe, and the denunciations of the Apocalypse were provoked. Paul begged the Philippians to exercise their Roman citizenship as Christians should (Phil. 1:27), and he himself set the example. One of the purposes of Luke's second "treatise" (see Acts 1:1, KJV) was to establish the fact that the new faith was no subversive doctrine, and the Church no alien state within the State (see Rom. 13:1-7).

The great Augustus had sought, by a revival of the old moralities of Italian religion, to discover a cement for the empire. The cult of Caesar-worship and the adoration of the Spirit of Rome was a movement encouraged especially in the favorable soil of the eastern Mediterranean with the same end in view. Rome had her supreme opportunity to find in Christianity the consolidating force her wiser instincts, as an imperial power, sought. It was due to the mad young Nero's foolishness and fear, after the Great Fire of July 64, that this enormous historic chance was lost.

It was "for the Lord's sake" (v. 13) that Peter ordered this, and the phrase expresses not only the political wisdom which grew so amazingly in minds illuminated by God, but also because the Lord himself had bidden them to give to Caesar that which was Caesar's due. Peter knew well enough that the provincial governors and the local magistrates appointed or recognized by Rome were neither infallible in the dispensing of justice, nor prodigal in rewarding good behavior, but both functions were ideally part of their office, and Peter writes as a Christian should.

Such conduct, he maintains, while certainly the will of God, would play its part in silencing the criticism of slanderous men. The source of the riot at Ephesus was falsehood propagated by a manufacturer of heathen souvenirs for the pilgrim trade whose pocket was hit by the preaching of a pure religion. The letters of Pliny to Trajan, written in A.D. 111 to ask the emperor's advice about the Christian influence in Bithynia, also illustrate the reality of slander in patterns of imperial repression.

Pliny had taken trouble to investigate and found that the hostile criticism was based both on malice and ignorance. The word Peter uses translated "put to silence" is that of Matthew 22:34.

Christians are "free" (John 8:36; Gal. 2:4), but Peter knew of the heresy which could be made of Paul's doctrine of freedom. Peter knew what had happened in Corinth and Galatia. A dangerous minority in the Church had received the gospel as a system of liberal philosophy, a scheme of emancipation which broke the bondage of old taboos, not indeed to replace them with the higher loyalties and loftier standards of Christian love but with a license which dishonored Christ. Paul had taught that prohibitions were abolished for the righteous. Those who distorted his doctrine, "ill-informed and unbalanced people," as 2 Peter 3:16 describes them, maintained that all things were lawful to the redeemed. "The law is dead" was their motto, and they made their liberty an occasion for the flesh. This danger lies in the bold Pauline gospel. Those who originally challenged Paul on this issue had such evidence as the disorderly church at Corinth provided to prove their point. And that evidence might be multiplied.

"Right through Christian history," writes J. S. Stewart in *A Man in Christ* (London: Hodder & Stoughton, 1930; reprint ed. Grand Rapids, Mich.: Baker, 1975, pp. 194–97), "the workings of this spirit can be traced; men have found it easy to shelter their sins beneath 'the imputed righteousness of Christ,' have used a phrase like 'not under the law but under grace' to blur the otherwise disturbing fact that God is holy and that there is such a thing as the moral stringency of Jesus. . . . So the Christian faith has been wounded in the house of its friends, and the terribly damaging divorce between religion and ethics casts a slur on the Church's name. . . ." Hence Peter's warning. They were free, but responsible.

> Honor all men. Love the brotherhood. Reverence God and honor the emperor. Slaves, subject yourselves to your masters with all respect, not only the good and kindly ones but also the harsh ones. For there is grace in this if a man, because he is conscious of God, endures wrong, though he suffers it unjustly. What credit is there in enduring a thrashing when you do wrong? But if when you do well, and still suffer, you endure it, this is grace in the sight of God (2:17–20).

Christianity was to destroy slavery but it was part of the wisdom of the apostles to allow the force and power of Christian love to work the social transformation. The social benefits of the faith are byproducts which flow effectively only from men transformed. Great reforms must rise from the roots implanted in the personality of man. Ancient society, bound economically to the hateful institution of slavery, would have lapsed into chaos at a sudden change, even if there were any means by which it could have been brought about. Roman history had known slave revolts, but the Christian Church had no mandate to bring about revolution and bloodshed. It preached peace. Nor could the Christian minority challenge the State in a manner which could only have precipitated reprisal, repression and defeat. The Christian doctrine of the love of God and the value of the human personality cut slavery at the root, and ensured its ultimate withering away. That is why Paul sent Onesimus back to his master, and Paul's clear hint to Philemon is an anticipation of things to come.

Meanwhile the slave had an opportunity to testify, a somber and difficult task, but implicit in his allegiance to God. Peter clearly has in mind the Lord's words in Luke 6:32. We have kept the word *grace* in the translation, remembering J. B. Phillips's rendering of the word in John 1:16 ". . . grace in our lives because of his grace."

> For it was to this kind of life that you were called, because Christ too suffered on our behalf, leaving you an example that you should follow in his steps—he who did no sin nor was deceit found in his mouth; he who, when he was reviled, offered no reviling in return, when he suffered made no threats, but left himself in the hands of him who judges righteously; who himself bore our sins in his own body

on the tree, that we, dead to our sins, should live for righteousness, and it was by his wounding you were healed. For you were like straying sheep but you have now returned to the Shepherd and Guardian of your souls (2:21–25).

It is a solemn fact, too often forgotten by the purveyors of common forms of experiential and emotional Christianity, that Christians are called to the sort of life Christ lived, in the sense that his attitudes, and often his suffering, are commonly worked out in the patterns of daily life. To live like Christ often means to confront what Christ confronted, and he warned his followers of that possibility as early as the Beatitudes.

An "example" (v. 21) was a copybook heading, or a traced series of letters or words over which the pupil wrote, or which he sought exactly to reproduce. In a difficult passage from the *Protagoras*, Plato mentions the practice, but the description is obscure. However, with reference to the Platonic passage, Quintilian refers to letters traced on wax tablets and children learning to write by following the marks with a stylus "as though along furrows." Peter's word *hupogramma* means literally an "underwriting," so something of an exact imitation is implied.

Peter then slips into the language of Isaiah 53, possibly in a form found in catechistic formulations of the Early Church teachers. Peter had vivid and painful memories of the trial of Christ—the insults, the threats, and the superb and silent dignity with which, on that awful night, he had met the spite of men. This passage, remember, was addressed to slaves. Christ is offered as their example. Already we see the leaven at work. A slave was a chattle, a "speaking tool," denied personality, a mere thing. Aristotle in the passage just quoted says: "There can be no friendship or justice towards inanimate things; indeed not even towards a horse or an ox, nor yet towards a slave as such. Master and slave have nothing in common; a slave is a living tool, just as a tool is an inanimate slave."

Such philosophic theorizing did not always govern conduct. Human nature sometimes broke through for good, and there were slaves who were loved and esteemed. But consider what Peter here does. He draws the slave into the fellowship of the Son of God. His example was theirs. It was bound to stir humanity to life. We, he says, including slaves and free in one brotherhood (vv. 17, 24), have been lifted from death to life by the death of Christ—Christ dead on such an instrument of horror and torture as Rome reserved for delinquent slaves. Nothing could more effectively give the downtrodden dignity.

The section closes with a beautiful image (v. 25). The figure of the shepherd is as old as Scripture. Indeed, it is older. From the records of the

Euphrates Valley and the century of Abraham emerges the story of a strangely attractive person, Kudur-Mabug, king of Elam, who saved the city of Larsam from an Amorite attack. The brief telling of his exploit ascribes glory to God, and prays that he may be a "dear shepherd" to his people. From Moses and the Shepherd Psalm, and on to the Lord's description of himself, the image runs. We, foolish, wandering, prone blindly to follow any leader into peril, have one who guards and keeps. And the image must be viewed in the context of Eastern and ancient shepherding, not in the context of the droving and mustering of today.

The word translated "guardian" is *episkopos*, from which the word *bishop* derives. Its primary meaning is "overseer," and the word goes back to Hector, the Trojan hero who held the "oversight" of the folk of Troy. In the island republic of Rhodes the *episkopoi* were the ruling group of five magistrates. It was a word of strength and high authority.

··{3}··

For Christians in the Home

In the same manner, you wives, be in submission to your own husbands, so that if any are not obedient to the word they may be won by their wives' mode of living without a word, having before their eyes your chaste, respectful mode of life. Let your adornment not be that outward adornment of braiding of hair, wearing of gold, and putting on of clothes, but rather the inner person revealed in what cannot be destroyed, a gentle and serene spirit, something precious in the eyes of God. For so the good women of the past, who put their hope in God, would adorn themselves, being in submission to their own husbands. Sarah is an example, who obeyed Abraham, calling him master. And you are her daughters, if you do well and let nothing daunt you (3:1–6).

The chapter division is a little artificial because Peter is still preoccupied with the theme of Christian behavior in the household. It is obvious that a major problem arose, as it still does, if a woman became a Christian while her husband was unconvinced. In an ancient context a husband had enough authority, if he was the Christian partner, to take it for granted that his wife would at least accompany him in his fellowship with the Christian group. The reverse did not necessarily apply. Hence, the more detailed advice to the wives. Paul similarly dealt with this very real problem (Eph. 5:21–24; Col. 3:18; Titus 2:4). Neither Peter nor Paul saw in the situation a call or excuse for the dissolution of a marriage. It merely placed a heavy burden on the female partner.

Talk, Peter saw, was of small value. The daily presence of a woman obviously transformed, who makes no loud parade of her faith, but presents a spectacle of pure goodness, can be more compelling than any amount of speech. The whole social pattern is, of course, in view. It was a male society, and within that context Peter wrote. Women found a charter in the gospel. For all the allegations to the contrary, Paul acknowledges his debt to women, and more than once expresses his reverence and admiration for their work and ministrations. Peter is merely facing reality. Women among the Greeks were not expected to be noisy (1 Cor. 14:34). "Silence is the proper adornment for women," says Ajax to poor Tecmessa in Sophocles's play (*Ajax* 293).

The rabbis also had many words to say on the subject, words reprehensible often enough, but facts of life which the Church had to take into account if a Christian woman's lot was not to be unbearable and her desire to win her husband frustrated. Besides, divorce was easy, loaded in the husband's favor, and a peril, if possible, to be avoided. Rules may have been formulated. Peter and Paul obviously teach in congruent fashion (1 Cor. 7:13–16).

Peter simply directs the Christian woman to do what lies in her control to do—be a good wife. The command to be submissive suggests that the vision of freedom implicit in Christianity (1 Pet. 2:16) was promoting restiveness, not only among slaves, but also among married women. It is natural enough that a new and thrilling notion of the importance of the human personality, and that Christ died to give it life and meaning, should engender feelings of revolt against any form of servitude. Peter calls women to patience, voluntary submissiveness, and very real self-sacrifice. If the wife's first thought is to be, as Peter assumed it necessarily had to be, her husband's conversion, then there was only one course open—the impact on a disobedient life of an obedient soul. The translation uses the adjectives "chaste, respectful" to describe this life, but could have used "chaste, reverent." *Respectful* would direct the thought to the wife's attitude in the home. She treats her husband with courteous regard. *Reverent* would speak of an attitude towards God. The result would be identical.

Peter goes on to deal with female adornment of dress. The context again must be kept in mind. There is no direction here to a modern Christian woman to wear somber garments, shun ornament or damage comeliness by austere hair styling. The principles nonetheless apply, and equally to men as to women. Gaudiness or extravagance of dress, or any form of adornment which attracts the comment of a critic for its absurdity, expense or exhibitionist fashion, is no commendation for Christ. The Old Testament prophets marked down female ornamentation as the mark of ostentatious affluence, unworthy of those who worship God (Isa. 3:18–24). The courtesans of the obscene fertility cults were also marked by their hair style and dress. When Jezebel met her end, she adorned herself and went to the window, no doubt assuming the role of such a priestess in defiance of her foes.

Both Roman and Greek saw ethical implications in women's dress. The Senate legislated on the subject in the sterner days of Rome's Republic. Under the empire, as many statues show, female emancipation had led to elaborate hair styling. Juvenal and Plutarch, writing half a century after Peter, speak vehemently against flashy and vulgar female ornament and dress. Plutarch, in fact, uses the very word for adornment which Peter uses, and maintains that gold and pearls really add nothing to true beauty. Gravity, decorum and modesty, on the other hand, do. Plutarch wisely adds that it is good for husbands to set a proper example. Peter therefore was sharing the views of his times, and in the Early Church generally women accepted them. Monica, the saintly mother of Augustine of Hippo, who died in A.D. 387, is an illustration. In the Ninth Book of the *Confessions*, Augustine tells of Monica's death and describes how she won her pagan husband to Christ before he died, "by the message of her character, whereby God made her beautiful to him, reverently lovable, and wonderful."

Be like Sarah, said Peter. He has Isaiah 51:2 in mind. And then, remembering Paul (Rom. 7:22), he continued: "It is the hidden man, the heart" which matters (v. 4. literal). The puzzling last phrase of verse 6 deprecating fear seems to refer to Sarah's sudden terror at God's rebuke. Ronald Knox renders: ". . . and let no anxious thoughts disturb you." Perhaps it is a general exhortation to confidence, a quality not easily attained amid the chronic insecurity of such a household as Peter has in mind.

One thought, however, does emerge. In a beautifully written story in Genesis, Abraham sends his servant Eliezer of Damascus round the Fertile Crescent trade route to Haran to find a bride for his son Isaac. He sent rich ornaments, "jewels of silver, and jewels of gold, and raiment," which were given to Rebecca (Gen. 24:53). It seems unlikely that

Rebecca's future mother-in-law would have remained unadorned during her life, beautiful woman though she was—if we are to credit the Genesis documents from Qumran.

All such matters are to be seen in social, historical and even geographical contexts. Corinth is a case in point, and the direction about the covering of the head, relevant there, probably applied nowhere else. The obvious need is one John Wesley put succinctly: "As to matters of dress, I would recommend one not to be first in the fashion, nor the last out of it." Dress should not, either by its slovenliness or by its ostentation, divert attention from the person, and the One to whom he necessarily bears witness. The divided household still exists, and a Christian can turn a non-Christian partner from Christ as readily by preoccupation with dress as by carelessness in it.

Another thought arises. Peter must have been writing for a church which contained the affluent as well as the poor—a matter clear from James and the list of names in the Pauline epistles. The sneer of Gibbon already referred to, that the Christian community was composed of "the dregs of the populace," slaves, women, workmen and so on, is very far from the truth. The group to whom Peter's exhortation in this section was addressed was just such a cross section of society as the Church still shows— made one, made equal by their faith. Some who heard this pastoral letter read might smile ironically at the strictness on jewelry. Others might go home, look with new misgiving in their Corinthian bronze mirrors, and decide to dress more modestly, less provocatively, and more in tune with a womanly reserve.

Perhaps Benjamin Franklin was as wise when he framed the precept: "Eat to please yourself, but dress to please others." A properly groomed spirit will express itself in becoming clothes, as surely as, in Josh Billings's quaint phrase, "clothes are the intellect of the dandy." And was it not Thomas Hardy who described someone, in language more earthy than verse 4, as "a singular framework of clothes, with nothing of any consequence inside them"?

In the same manner, you husbands be understanding in your lives together, remembering that your wives are the weaker sex, but giving them honor as your equal partners in the grace of life, so that the two of you will not be hindered in your prayers.

To sum up, be of one mind, compassionate to one another in brotherly love, tenderhearted, humble-minded, not returning evil for evil, or abuse for abuse, but on the contrary blessing, for it was to this you were called—to obtain a part in blessing. For, "One who would love life and see good days, let him restrain his tongue from evil and his lips from speaking deceitfully. Let him shun evil and do good, let him seek peace and follow after it, for the eyes of the Lord are upon the good, and his ears attentive to their prayers. The face of the Lord is against evil-doers" (3:7–12).

Turning to husbands, Peter stresses the fact that married life is no hindrance to devotion. He is no advocate of a pious celibacy. Phillips's colloquial translation puts the injunction well: "Similarly, you husbands should try to undersand the wives you live with, honoring them as physically weaker yet equally heirs with you of the grace of life. If you don't do this, you will find it impossible to pray properly." Here is the way to domestic harmony, and absence of such harmony makes an atmosphere inimical to prayer. A tense and unhappy married life and a disordered home can destroy devotion and consistent prayer. Paul touched the same thought with a compelling analogy in Ephesians 5:24.

To sum up, Peter concludes in verse 8, let us exercise the brotherly qualities of love, sympathy, generosity, and courtesy, never capping malice with malice, never meeting insult with insult. Rather let it be the contrary, for we who are the heirs of blessing should be quick to bless (v. 9). From the list in verse 8 let us select the quality of compassion or sympathy. Peter echoes Paul again, for this is the thought of Romans 12:15. *Compassion*, or its synonym *sympathy*, is the faculty of entering into the feelings of another. "He watched and wept, he prayed and felt for all," said Oliver Goldsmith of his village parson in *The Deserted Village*. Sympathy is a virtue unknown outside of man, for it is a fragment of the image of God in which man was made. It drew the tears of Christ. Sympathy refrains from the word which hurts and the deed which harms. It bears the burdens of others and seeks at cost of pain to share grief and distress. It is outreaching love. It is, as Edmund Burke put it, "next to love the divinest passion of the human heart."

The following verses (10–13) are a free quotation, used as a hymn or psalm of the Early Church. So some translations print the words—Phillips, for example—as poetry:

> He that would love life,
> And see good days,
> Let him refrain his tongue from evil,
> And his lips that they speak no guile:
> And let him turn away from evil, and do good;
> Let him seek peace and pursue it.
> For the eyes of the Lord are upon the righteous,
> And his ears unto their supplication:
> But the face of the Lord is against them that do evil.

Note the balance of phrasing proper to the Hebrew concept of poetry, the verbal patterning of the psalms.

The words of this hymn or psalm come from the society which was "hated for its crimes," as the misinformed words of the historian Tacitus described Nero's victims, the Christians of Rome in A.D. 64.

Such slander fell on our forefathers in the faith. It fell on Christ. Should we be surprised at human misunderstanding? It is for us to be sure that our tongue is bridled. "What word is this," a character in Homer says, "which has escaped the barrier of your teeth?" The lips can be, in truth, the first exit of indwelling evil. Speech is the prime tool of deceit, as Peter suggests, and the penalty for deceit is to deceive oneself. Nathaniel Hawthorne remarked: "No man, for any considerable period wears one face to himself and another to the multitude without finally becoming bewildered as to which may be true." And hatred of guile is as old as Homer, who makes Achilles say:

> Who dares think one thing and another tell,
> My heart detests him as the gates of hell.

For who is going to harm you if you are eager to do good. And happy you are if you suffer for righteousness. Do not fear their intimidation, nor be distressed, but revere the Lord Christ in the depths of your being, ever ready to give an answer to anyone who asks you about the hope you hold—but with gentleness and reverence. Maintain a good conscience, so that those who revile your good Christian life may be put to shame in the very sphere in which they slander you. For it is better, if God so will, to suffer for doing good than for doing evil (3:13–17).

Peter first expresses an ideal—but ideals seldom conform to reality. Peter knew as much from his own experience and from that of his Master. He remembers again the Sermon on the Mount and continues. In spite of all, it may still come about that the Christian is harmed and persecuted (v. 14). Evil is abroad in the world, and corruption finds harbor in the hearts of men, and no more can be expected. Christ suffered—he who knew no sin. Can the follower of Christ expect less? The familiar pattern runs through history. "Crucify him . . . away with him . . . not this man but Barabbas . . . he has a devil . . . a gluttonous man and a winebibber. . . ." That is what John Bunyan had in mind when he described in *Pilgrim's Progress* the packed jury for Faithful's trial in Vanity Fair.

"Then said Mr. No-Good, Away with such a fellow from the earth. Ay, said Mr. Malice, for I hate the very looks of him. Then said Mr. Lovelust, I could never endure him. Nor I, said Mr. Live-loose, for he would ever be condemning my way. . . . A sorry scrub! said Mr. High-mind."

The smell of the martyr's fires, flesh burning, the reek of man's intolerance to man, fill the human story. Man will not have before his eyes the reproach of human goodness, if by stone, stick, sword, or slave-camp he can thrust it out of sight. And those periods of tolerance which have imag-

ined that such evil has at last been purged have
ended always like our own sinister century in sharp
awakening.

Yet the duty of testimony, intelligent and clear
testimony, abides—not always an easy task. The
English reserve in us dislikes parade and the display
in public of intimate convictions. Courtesy, good
breeding, humility itself, revolts from exhibitionism
and the appearance of self-righteousness. It is a century since the Earl of Shaftesbury ventured the
opinion that "men of sense are really but of one
religion," and that "men of sense never tell it.
. . ." On the other hand, Peter here commands:
"Be ready at any time to give a quiet and reverent
answer to any man who wants a reason for the hope
that you have within you" (v. 15). There are times
of brash challenge when a Christian must speak up.
In so doing he claims no special excellence. He
merely bears witness to what a faith has meant to
him and seeks to share that which has made life real
and purposeful and has built his mind's tranquility.

But how? Not with arrogance, cocksureness,
boasting, crudity or any shadow of self-righteousness. It must be done, says the KJV, with "meekness
and fear." It is interesting to look at the modern
versions. "With modesty and respect" (NEB)
touches courtesy's need to be gentle with another's
point of view. "Gently and cautiously," says Weymouth, less happily, for caution is not the mood.

"Courteously and with due reverence," says Knox.

However we may answer, let us be prepared, by Bible study and thoughtful meditation, and a sensitive awareness of opportunity obviously put in our way. Peter clearly has in mind something more than the testimony of words. He values the personal encounter of a quiet and courteous man above what can be said. There will be many who will be daunted and shamed by the evident goodness of those they have slandered. It can hardly be denied that it was the manner of life of the first Christians which, more than any preaching, caught the attention of the pagan world. They were indeed "the only Bible a careless world will read." They were "the sinner's Gospel," they were "the scoffer's Creed."

Seneca, the philosopher and teacher who tutored Nero and whom Nero drove to suicide, had said in Rome a few years before Peter wrote: "Men trust rather to their eyes than to their ears. The effect of precepts is therefore slow and tedious, while that of examples is summary and effectual. . . . Noble examples stir us up to noble actions and the very history of large and public souls inspires a man with generous thoughts."

At the same time Christians must tell in whose Name they do what they do, and in what faith and hope they become what they are. Testimony of speech and character must be congruent and intertwined.

Christ himself died for sins, once for all, the just for the unjust, to bring us near to God—he who was put to death in the flesh, but brought to life in the spirit. And it was in the spirit that he made proclamation to the spirits in prison, those who were disobedient at the time when God's patience endured in the days of Noah, when the ark was being prepared, in which a few, eight in fact, were brought safely through the water (3:18–20).

Verse 18 contains a phrase of Peter's. He uses it in Acts 3:14—a messianic title found in the Book of Enoch, "the Just One." Verses 19 and 20 form probably the most difficult passage to explain in the whole New Testament. In 1 Peter 4:6 there is a similar and related puzzle. It is probable that there is no satisfactory interpretation of these passages available. It is too commonly a preoccupation of commentators to set down at all costs some interpretation for every difficult passage in the Bible. But it surely does not insult Scripture humbly to admit that there may be contexts to which the key is lost or not yet found. The teacher of Scripture is under no obligation to explain everything, and to claim ability to do so would touch the edge of absurdity.

A good case can be made, though a far from conclusive one, for Moffatt's emendation, following a suggestion by Rendel Harris. A small textual change would make the verse read: "It was in the Spirit that Enoch also went and preached to imprisoned spirits. . . ." This, of course, only replaces one difficulty by another and also incurs the charge of accepting without any manuscript support a plausible emendation of a text to avoid an exegetical difficulty—always a temptation to the commentator. But Enoch has crossed Peter's mind (v. 18).

But there still remains the question of the identity of "the spirits in prison." The Church Fathers believed that "the disobedient" were in the first case the doomed of Noah's generation, and that these were typical of all who lived before the coming of a Savior. The Eastern Church especially believed that Christ, free from the body but not yet resurrected, visited this multitude in some place of confinement, and offered them salvation. Others see in the phrase the fallen angels, or those beings who seduced man before the Flood (Gen. 6:1–7).

Neither explanation seems satisfactory, but Peter is hurrying on to a word about baptism and mentions the descent of Christ to the world of the dead only in passing, and evidently in the confidence that those who heard him knew what he was speaking about. Evidently he is again moving in a pattern of thinking alien to us but familiar enough to him and his. In this case, however, we cannot turn to Old Testament texts (as in the case of his sustained metaphor of "the Cornerstone") to elucidate his meaning. It is better to confess that the full meaning eludes us, and to remember that, had not this passage become a subject of such common speculation at the time when Christian creeds were taking shape, it would not now be so well-known. The misleading English of "He descended into hell" quite unnecessarily adds words to the Creed, but also creates difficulties of understanding and belief which need not have arisen.

One fact of prime importance does, however, emerge. This passage was written, again let us stress, by one who saw the living Christ, who entered the empty tomb and "saw the linen clothes lying. . . ." No man could write even these difficult words save one who had no shadow of doubt about the death of Christ and his bodily resurrection. This was no purveyor of myth, no trafficker in symbols, no visionary building a structure of legend round a mystic sense of a Presence, "mocking God with metaphor." It was a man who knew some historical facts which were for him beyond argument.

> It was this event, which was a prefiguring of baptism, by which you are brought to salvation today, something more than a washing off of the body's dirt, but the appeal of a good conscience to God, through the resurrection of Jesus Christ who has gone to heaven and is on the right hand of God, with angels, powers and authorities made subject to him (3:21–22).

Peter is not preaching any form of "baptismal regeneration." He has enough to say in his letters and sermons to make it clear that, like Paul, he believes that it is by faith that a man is saved. But what is baptism save an expression and a confession of that faith? And faith necessarily contained the belief in a historic resurrection? It was that event which made faith significant, gave faith basis and hope. Faith meant from the very beginning confidence in Christ's living power to pardon sin and give new life.

Peter seems to be advancing the new Christian view of baptism. It is something more than the ceremonial washing of rabbinical ritual, lifted to a new height by "the Baptist," and already used mystically by Paul (Eph. 5:26) and later by the writer to the Hebrews (Heb. 10:22). He seems to suggest that the act of baptism meant a rising to new life, a conscience which could come unashamed before God. Just as the flood, for its survivors, was a resurrection (Rom. 6:1–13), a passing through death into new life, so was baptism for the Christian. Paul, following a similar train of Hebrew thinking, had used the crossing of the Red Sea (1 Cor. 10:1, 2).

The point to stress in this passage is that newness of life was the insistence of the early Christians, a matter which impressed the governor of Bithynia who reported to the Emperor Trajan on the Christians in A.D. 111. His private agents who investigated the Christians reported that they were no subversive organization, but a harmless community who worshiped Christ as God and "bound themselves by an oath not to commit theft or robbery or adultery and not to deny the receipt of money when demanded." This was a down-to-earth rendering of "a clear conscience." (Those interested in a scholarly and closely argued account of this passage and its context should look at Dr. G. R. Beasley-Murray's exhaustive survey *Baptism in the New Testament* [Exeter: Paternoster Press, 1972; Grand Rapids, Mich.: Eerdmans, 1973.])

For the remainder of the paragraph it should be noted that the royal metaphor of the enthroned Christ is a recognizable phrase of Peter (Acts 2:32–35). The supremacy of Christ over all manner of authority was a thought more than once expressed by Paul (1 Cor. 15:24–28; Eph. 1:28). Peter reminds Christians bowed by the burden of imperial authority, soon to turn to official repression, that they have a supreme guardian.

··{4}··

For Christians
in a Day of Crisis

Since Christ, then, suffered in his human body, do
you, too, arm yourselves with the same resolve, for
the one who has suffered in his body has ceased from
sin, to live for the rest of his earthly life, not for the
things that men desire but as God wills. Your past
life is long enough to have been doing what pagans
like to do, living lives of sensuality, lust, drunkenness, wild parties, drinking bouts, and profane idola-
try. This is where they think it odd that you do not
run along with them into the same welter of dissipation . . . (4:1–4a).

The first verse can be best understood in reference
to Romans 6:1–14, where baptism is mystically explained as a kind of sharing with Christ a death and
a resurrection. The whole passage in Paul's closely
argued chapter should be studied on the assumption
that Peter's thought had been deeply penetrated by
it. Nor is that important passage to be read as an
abstruse tract of mere theological significance. Both
Paul and Peter see practical application in the

thought of death and resurrection for all who have been thus born to new life. The whole psychology of Christian living is found in the firm conviction that there are old ways of life and carnality to which the Christian should doggedly consider himself dead, and new aspirations, urges, and desires to which, with equal fervor, he should consider himself alive.

The redeemed then have "died to sin" in the person of Christ (Rom. 6:10, RSV). "Look upon yourselves," runs J. B. Phillips's rendering of Romans 6:11, "as dead to the appeal and power of sin but alive and sensitive to the call of God through Jesus Christ our Lord." The practice of Christian self-discipline could not be better expressed. The studied, firm denial of expression to evil impulses is replaced by a careful promotion and cultivation of every urge to good. No vacuum of repression is left. This is the psychologist's "sublimation" in the finest sense of the word. There is no empty habitation, "swept, and garnished," as the perceptive little parable of Christ had it (Matt. 12:44, KJV), waiting to be reoccupied by a swarm of the old tenants. There is a new occupier, the Spirit of the living God. The personality thus possessed is not passive but active with desire for good and with God's will monopolizing all awareness.

Thus, says Peter, on the same theme, remembering that Christ died for us, let us turn from a fruitless past to a fruitful future. "You had time enough in the past to do all the things that men want to do in the pagan world . . ." (v. 3, NEB). He proceeds to list the common excesses of the flesh. They are familiar enough, for the world of such desires is still the world of multitudes. The "wild parties" (LB) probably include the orgiastic rites associated in the first century with some exotic pagan cults. Illustration may be found in the wall paintings of Pompeii, in the "House of the Mysteries," for example. The "drinking bouts" may have similar significance, perhaps some connection with the guild-feasts which haunt the background of the first letter to Corinth. In that disordered church, of course, drunkenness at the Lord's table was not unknown.

Verse 4 faces a familiar fact. "Your former companions may think it queer that you will no longer join with them . . ." (Phillips). The reaction of society to a Christian's stand for righteousness is too often, thanks to one of the more contemptible facets of human nature, resentment and malice. Many a lonely boy in an army camp, a girl in a students' hostel, or a Christian family in some close-knit suburban group, has known the open or the covert persecution of the conforming majority. Normal men and women do not enjoy dissent and withdrawal from surrounding society. It is a natural, and indeed a harmless, human instinct to wish to do at Rome as Rome does. But if Rome, as ancient Rome once did, turns with vicious malice against good men and women who refuse to conform to its carnality and godlessness, one course only is open— to remember the Holy One whom Rome destroyed, and stand firm in spite of all.

The word rendered "dissipation" (v. 4) is the Greek noun *asotia*. It appears in adverbial form in the story of the Prodigal Son (Luke 15:13) for the "riotous living" with which he "wasted his substance" (KJV). Similar derivatives occur in Ephesians 5:18 and Titus 1:6. There is a papyrus fragment also containing the related verb, where two exasperated parents refuse responsibility for debts contracted by their son's dissipation.

> Thus they blaspheme, but they shall give due account to the One who is ready to judge the living and the dead (4:4b–5).

The fourth verse ends with a participle, recognizable if transliterated (*blasphemountes*), but not too easy to translate. In the above translation it has simply been taken literally to mean that in the very act of finding strange or ludicrous the transformed life of Christians, cynical pagans dishonor the name of him who has wrought the change. The word, however, from Classical to New Testament Greek, can mean to defame or revile a person (Titus 3:2 and Romans 3:8 are examples). The related noun, similarly, can signify slander and defamation (Mark 7:22 and Ephesians 4:31 are examples).

This may well be the meaning here, for Peter has had something to say already about the pagan misrepresentation of Christians and the slander invented against them. Let the persecutor know that he will one day be judged, here or hereafter.

> Though the mills of God grind slowly, yet they
>   grind exceeding small;
> Though with patience He stands waiting, with
>   exactness grinds He all.
> —Friedrich von Logau, translated by
>   Henry Wadsworth Longfellow

This is why the gospel was preached to the dead also that, though judged in the flesh as men are judged, they might live in the spirit as God lives. The end of everything is near. . . . (4:6–7a).

The mystery of this preresurrection ministry of Christ (v. 6) eludes explanation. The subject was opened in chapter 3, and there is no avoiding the fact that no one can completely explain Peter's words. William Barclay greets the verse with delight, as one of the most wonderful statements in the Bible. "It gives," he says, "a breathtaking glimpse of nothing less than a gospel of a second chance." No one will deny that this, indeed, would be "good news," from the standpoint of human ignorance, at least. It is impossible, however, to support it by any other passage of Scripture, and the whole weight of the New Testament is against the possibility that any who consciously reject Christ in this life have any opportunity to reconsider their choice in another. Peter himself would repudiate the idea. The words are better left without explanation. Peter knew what he meant. Those who heard or read his letter knew what he meant. We do not, because we have lost some piece of relevant information or some vital clue.

The first half of verse 7 is to be carefully considered. "The end of everything is near." This is a note struck elsewhere (Rom. 13:12; Phil. 4:5; James 5:8; 1 John 2:18; Rev. 1:3, 22:20). John wrote thirty years after Peter died, and it was not the obstinacy of an old man in his nineties which still sustained the thought that the end was near. In the widest significance of the word, Paul, Peter, James, John were writing in "the last hour" in truth. The only event in all history which can equal in significance the First Coming of Christ must be the Second Coming. And what are twenty centuries compared even with the age of the galaxy? Calvin comments correctly: "He calls that 'the last time' in which all things are so completed that nothing is left except the last revelation of Christ."

It is the common fashion to dismiss tracts of the New Testament as irrelevant because, it is alleged, they were written under the mistaken assumption that the end of the age was at hand. It is over sixty years since the well-known humanitarian Albert

Schweitzer attempted his interpretation of the Lord's life and death on such principles in a perverse and mistaken work which was not accepted by many theological liberals, besides being rejected roundly by conservative scholars. In 1912, two years after the general rejection of his earlier thesis, Schweitzer attempted to apply his ideas to the ministry of Paul, only to fail more demonstrably. Schweitzer appears to have recognized the fact, for in 1913, having taken his medical degree, he went to Lambarene and to a wide reputation as a somewhat eccentric missionary in medical and social work. It is strange to find his perverse theological ideas still quoted today.

In point of fact, a matter stressed in the introduction, if not the end of a world, the end of an age was indeed upon the Church. Gone, within a few short years, was all security, all hope that the empire would prove sympathetic to the gospel; gone all the little safe and prosperous world of thousands of innocent and good Christian people. A line runs through Roman history in A.D. 64. It marks the empire's rejection of Christ, the end of a chapter, if not of the book. And Peter's timeless words have been read in the dire context of many another chapter ending.

With this in mind, discipline yourselves, and practice self-control to aid your prayers. Above all keep your loving fellowship constant, for love covers a host of sins. Use hospitality towards one another without grumbling. Whatever endowment each one has received, use it in service to one another like careful trustees of God's varied grace. If anyone speaks, let it be the words of God. If anyone serves others, let it be in the strength which God freely gives, that God in all things may be glorified through Jesus Christ, to whom is glory and power forever and ever. Amen (4:7b–11).

The Christian must therefore live with that alertness which is born of expectation. And this is shown in no wrapt contemplation of heavenly things but in the practical and mundane affairs of life. "He'll find me pickin' cotton when he comes," runs the negro spiritual, and Peter develops that theme. In the shadow of looming persecution and utter disaster, he bids his Christian flock first to face the menace in quiet prayerfulness: "Steady then, keep cool, and pray!" (v. 7), runs Moffatt's audacious but perfectly legitimate rendering. (Print it on a card and put it where you will often see it.)

Second, and with equal simplicity, he bids them maintain the unity which can be born out of love. Practical as ever, he tells them that this unity finds manifestation and convincing illustration in plain hospitality in the church community: "keep open house for all with a glad heart" (NTBE). They are to carry on, each in his proper sphere of Christian service (v. 10). Finally, they are to preach the word, and nothing but the word, and serve with the full consciousness that the service is to God himself. . . . Could advice be more down to earth? We should live every day as if it were our last, or the last day of all. And this does not mean inactivity, but action—action directed to the tasks near the hand, and the sane, quiet fulfillment of the duties of the hour. So shall we glorify God, so most effectively testify, so be ready when he comes.

Look back over some of the incidental points. "Love covers a multitude of sins" (v. 8, RSV) has puzzled commentators and translators. The Septuagint distorted the verse by mistranslating it "Love covers all who do not love strife." The Syriac version substituted "shame" for "love." The thought, however, emerges from Luke 7:47; James 5:20 has it in mind, and the notion may be traced back to Proverbs (10:12). There is, nonetheless, an elusive shift of meaning over the history of the words.

The Lord meant, surely, that one who truly loved him had demonstrated a genuine and saving repentance. And does James mean that one who can lead another to Christ gives evidence of the blotting out of the sins he has known and those which his convert has committed? And does Peter mean that love which is "always slow to expose, believes the best, is always hopeful" (1 Cor. 13:7, Moffatt) is an essential ingredient in a patient hospitality? Hospitality is to be Peter's next theme, and he is preparing the ground. Hospitality can be trying. It can strain fellowship to breaking point. It can be a hunting ground for hypocrites. John, later in the century, found it necessary to set certain limits (2 John). The *Didache*, or the *Teaching of the Twelve Apostles*, a document of early church rules which could be as ancient as the first century, actually limits the time a Christian traveler could stay with a host. It had a name for those who imposed on others—a *Christemporos*, or *Christ-trader*.

Hospitality, a fruit of fellowship, thus becomes naturally the theme. In that grim world of base and perilous lodging houses, it was one duty of Christians to make sure that travelers of their number had adequate protection on the roads. And travel was uncommonly active (see Acts 10:6, 21:6). Homes, too, with generous hospitality implied, were the only meeting places of the Christian Church (Rom. 16:5; 1 Cor. 16:19; Philem. 2).

Hence, the need for a generously open house and the accompanying tolerance required, for the Christian community contained people of widely different culture, race, ways of life, substance and assets. To mix at all levels without strain is not easy. The only solvent is love. Paul was equally insistent on hospitality as a virtue (Rom. 12:13; 1 Tim. 3:2, 5:10; Titus 1:8; Heb. 13:2 and Matt. 25:35, 43).

Then Peter turns to another Pauline theme (Rom. 12:3–8; 1 Cor. 12). There is a task for everyone, there are gifts for every person to exercise, contributions expected and due from each and every one. The trouble with the Church too often is that its members insist on functioning in manners and spheres for which they are not fitted. Paul's vivid metaphor of a properly integrated body underlines this truth. A Christian's talents, possessions, faculties and material goods are God's to use.

In verse 11 Peter speaks of the two major activities of the Church—preaching and service. Let the preacher, he continues, speak only the truth of God, with no private theme, no personal obsession corrupting the message. Let the person who seeks to serve do so, not in the strength of some enthusiasm of his own, but as God directs and energizes. In both activities, the object must be to bring men and women face to face with God and thereby bring them to repentance and surrender. Service, like preaching, should not conceal the name of him on whose behalf both tasks are undertaken. The final and overwhelming object is that God be glorified— that is to say, that his will may be done on earth, that the blessings he offers be known and received, that God should reign, "his kingdom come."

Beloved do not be surprised at the fiery trial which is coming to test you, as though some surprising thing had happened to you, but be glad in that you are sharing the sufferings of Christ, so that you may rejoice, too, triumphantly, when his glory is revealed. If you are reviled for the name of Christ, you are blessed because something of God's glory and God's spirit rests on you (4:12–14).

The Greek verb translated "be surprised" is found in participial form in the Athenian message to Paul (Acts 17:20—"strange things," KJV). The adjective is found in the subordinate clause "some surprising thing." In point of fact the KJV rendering is correct enough. This epistle is indeed very competently rendered in that version. It is simply necessary to maintain consistency throughout the verse ("be surprised," "surprising"; "think it not strange," "strange").

What was the fiery testing which Peter had in mind? The point at which imperial persecution officially began can be pinpointed, as we have seen, with some precision. July 64 saw the Great Fire of Rome, the occasion of Nero's panic-stricken pogrom against the Christian Church which was already strong and numerous in the capital. But already the Christians had been marked down as a dissident group, withdrawn from the common practices of the vicious society which their presence rebuked. Anyone in Rome, looking at the currents of life running through a dole-fed and undisciplined proletariat, could see that what happened in Ephesus could happen in Rome on an immensely wider front and in sanguinary cruelty. This in fact is what the Christians suffered at the mad young sadist's hand.

Nero himself was loose from the restraining hands of Seneca and Burrus, the former his old tutor, the other the commandant of the praetorian troops, Rome's household garrison. With Seneca's retirement in A.D. 62 and Burrus already dead, any observant man could see the trouble which burst on the empire in 68 and 69 already brewing. Anyone who also knew Palestine, where the cauldron was heating to the explosion of 66, must have realized that no Jew or Christian in the world could hope to escape the repercussions. Peter probably wrote with the horizons darkening at any time just before A.D. 64, the fateful year.

Remembering the Beatitudes, Peter besought his Christians to remember that they walked in the path of their Lord, and that in some moment of blessed confirmation, when all rebellion dies and man is brought to final recognition that Christ is Lord, all will be well. Peter had many words of his Master in mind (Matt. 10:24, 25; Mark 10:38, 39) and perhaps a cryptic word of Paul (Col. 1:24). With verse 14 and the signature word of the Beatitudes actually quoted ("happy," "blessed"), Peter underlines his texture of quotation. Persecution is hard to bear, but if it be borne in the name of Christ, and for no other reason than that the victim has affronted society because he is like his Lord, then something of a Shekinah glory (Exod. 16:7, 29:43, 40:34) lights upon him—a light about his brows which marks the presence of God.

It is moving to hear these words and imagine them read in small congregations of our ancestors in the faith just before the darkness fell. How far the congregations to whom Peter wrote were involved so early in the folly of Rome's repression we do not know. But if Peter wrote from Rome, the distant rumblings of a cruel storm were audible indeed.

> But let none of you suffer as a murderer, thief, evildoer, or as one who meddles in matters which have nothing to do with him. But if a man suffer because he is a Christian let him feel no shame, but in that name let him glorify God, for the time is here for judgment to begin at the house of God. And if our turn comes first, what shall be the end of those who reject the gospel of God? If it is hard for the good man to be saved, where shall the godless and the sinner appear? Therefore, let those who suffer because God has permitted it, commit their souls to their faithful Creator and continue to do good (4:15–19).

Conduct is again the theme. Of the 105 verses in this letter, 60 contain some reference to doctrine, and 65 touch on the conduct of the Christian in the home and in society. The crimes which Peter lists are those which the pagans alleged were tolerated among Christians. Tacitus, recounting Nero's persecution in the passage already quoted, speaks of the Christians' "hatred of the human race." And even when concluding his chapter with a comment on the final revulsion of the city proletariat against Nero's cruelty, the great historian, convinced by his authorities, says: "But guilty though these people were, and deserving of direst punishment, the fact that they were being sacrificed for no public good, but simply to glut the cruelty of one man, stirred some pity for them."

Pliny, too, the governor of Bithynia in A.D. 111, informing Trajan in the exchange of letters with the emperor on the subject of the Christians in the province, admits that he found nothing but good in them. Telling of the close examination he made, he writes:

"They affirmed, however, the whole of their guilt, or their error, was that they were in the habit of meeting on a certain fixed day before it was light, when they sang in alternate verses a hymn to Christ, as to a god, and bound themselves by a solemn oath, not to any wicked deed, but never to commit any fraud, theft or adultery, never to falsify their word, nor deny a trust when they should be called upon to deliver it up; after which it was their custom to separate, and then reassemble to partake of food— but food of an ordinary and innocent kind. Even this practice, however, they had abandoned after the publication of my edict, by which, according to your orders, I had forbidden political associations. I judged it so much the more necessary to extract the real truth, with the assistance of torture, from two female slaves, who were styled deaconesses: but I could discover nothing more than depraved and excessive superstition."

Speaking of the whole list of crimes Peter mentions (v. 15), R. J. Knowling in the *Expositor's Greek Testament* points out that the Lord suffered the fate reserved for murderers (Acts 3:14). He shared it with two thieves. He was delivered to Pilate as an evildoer (John 18:30). And he saved others; himself he could not save (Mark 15:31). The last crime mentioned is the only difficulty in the list. It is *allotriepiskopos* and the last half (*episkopos*) means an "overseer." (See comments on 2:25.) *Allotrios* means belonging to another. The meaning cannot be checked in any other context, for it occurs only in one other obscure passage in all surviving Greek literature. "Busybody" (KJV) is lamentably wrong. One who "infringes other men's rights," says Knox. A "mischief-maker," says the RSV.

The TCNT seems to have struck the most likely rendering: "for interfering in matters which do not concern Christians." This may be taken in two ways. First, perhaps Peter is deprecating Christian involvement in practices wrong in the eyes of the law, which might affect a man's testimony and justify slander. "Come out from among them," Paul had said, "and touch not the unclean thing" (2 Cor. 6:17, rsv). Secondly, carefully abstaining from mentioning anything to do with sedition, Peter may have been warning Christians, in a situation of growing peril, against involvement in plots against the regime. A major conspiracy against Nero was crushed in A.D. 65. There may have been many dissident groups at work. This was no time for Christians to be caught up in them. Social and political action are not thereby forbidden for Christians. All good is their affair. On the other hand, they have no right ever, or in any context, to be involved in movements which condone murder, theft or any sort of evildoing.

To suffer as a Christian is something different, and Paul agreed (2 Tim. 1:12). This is the third time in the New Testament in which the name *Christian* is mentioned. The term was invented in Antioch about A.D. 40–44, probably by a city official who noticed that there was a subgroup distinct from the mainly Jewish group of the synagogue and the ghetto. The Romans were expert in matters of census and population records, and the name made a convenient heading. It caught popular attention, and Agrippa used it naturally enough. Peter here accepts it, or else uses the term the persecutor would be likely to use. The opening paragraph of Pliny's letter already quoted uses the term in this sense.

"It is a rule, Sir, which I invariably observe, to

refer myself to you in all my doubts; for who is more capable of guiding my uncertainty or informing my ignorance? Having never been present at any trials of the Christians, I am unacquainted with the method and limits to be observed either in examining or punishing them. Whether any difference is to be made on account of age, or no distinction allowed between the youngest and the adult; whether repentance admits to a pardon, or if a man has been once a Christian it avails him nothing to recant; whether the mere profession of the name, albeit without crimes, or only the crimes associated therewith are punishable—in all these points I am greatly doubtful." Writing four or five years after Pliny of the events in Rome sixty years before, Tacitus also uses it, though whether this is evidence for the currency of the name in Nero's day cannot be said. From Peter's word it seems that this must be the case.

The coming ordeal of the Church was looked upon by its leader as a judgment. He has already described it as a testing (v. 12). It may be regarded as certain that the fire of persecution burned some dross and other alien intrusions out of the body of the Church. The thought of judgment beginning with the "household of God" (v. 17, RSV) is derived from Ezekiel 9:6 and is followed by a quotation from Proverbs 11:13, on which the strong and solemn medieval hymn, *Dies Irae*, is built. Peter, as

is commonly the case with New Testament writers,
follows the Septuagint version, a rendering closer to
the Lord's saying in Mark 10:24–26 which
prompted the question: "Who then can be saved?"
The memory of the words and doings of those three
tremendous years never left Peter's consciousness.

Verse 19 still applies. God does not *send* suffering
or *promote* persecution. Persecution is always and
always will be an evil, a vice devised by a godless
mind. God cannot be the author of any evil. On the
other hand, he does not always destroy evil or turn
it aside. He permits it. In such cases the Christians
must in God's name endure, and like Christ (Luke
23:46) commit their souls to God. The word translated "commit" is the word commonly applied to a
deposit—a sum of money or property of value placed
in trust with a reliable person, to be returned intact.
Pliny, in the letter quoted, reported that the sect
under investigation promised collectively and on
oath not to "deny a trust." Thus the persecuted
Christian promises to commit his life to God.

··{5}··

For Christians
in a Menaced Church

So to the elders of your number I address this
appeal, I who am an elder like you, and a witness of
the sufferings of Christ, a sharer too of the glory
which is yet to be revealed: Shepherd the flock of
God among you, not from a sense of duty, but will-
ingly, as God would have you do, not for some dis-
creditable profit, but eagerly, not flaunting your
authority over your charges, but showing yourselves
examples. And when the Chief Shepherd appears
you will receive a crown of glory which does not
fade (5:1–4).

Paul at this time was busy with his first letter to
Timothy and his letter to Titus. Both apostles were
obviously aware of the darkening skies and sought to
organize the Church to meet the darkness and to
establish strong systems of leadership. It is natural
enough that both great men should follow the patterns of government familiar in Jewish and Gentile
society. Rome had its *senate;* the word derives from

senex, an old man. This implies no advanced age but merely established seniority. The Greeks, too, were familiar enough with such experienced leadership.

The Jews traced their system of eldership back to the desert days (Num. 11:16–30). In the time of the kings, the elders formed a kind of council of state (1 Kings 20:8, 21:11 for example). Elders administered village communities and, in the Dispersion, led the synagogues. In the Gospels they are frequently mentioned along with priests, scribes and Pharisees (Matt. 16:21 for example). In the symbolism of the Apocalypse the elders sit, four and twenty, around the throne.

It is natural enough that the young Church should adopt and adapt a similar system, and in the story of the Church the system, familiar and functioning, is everywhere visible (Acts 11:30, 14:23, 15:2, 16:4, 20:7). Peter assumes its existence in the circuit of churches he has in view. His only concern is that the men who bore such a responsibility should be, like those Paul described at greater length, men of exemplary character. Seniority was generally the norm, but there could be exceptions (1 Tim. 4:12). What could not be set aside was uprightness, and, such is man, there were those who found in posts of leadership opportunity for gain. Paul uses Peter's word for "shameful gain" (v. 2, RSV) in Titus 1:7. Nor should they fall into that other vice of human pride, the love of petty power. This, the Lord had said (Matt. 20:25, 26), was a pagan custom, but alien to men of God. It is a ludicrous vice. Shakespeare had noted its pathos (*Measure for Measure*, Act 2, sc. 2, ll. 117–22):

> . . . man, proud man,
> Drest in a little brief authority,
> Most ignorant of what he's most assured,
> . . . .
> Plays such fantastic tricks before high heaven
> As make the angels weep. . . .

It seems ridiculous, but such usurpation and exhibitionism has damaged many a congregation. Peter has set an example. He calls himself not an apostle, but a fellow elder.

And the leaders of the churches are shepherds as he was. The whole passage is full of echoes which give it a ring of authenticity and truth. Peter had indeed witnessed the sufferings of Christ, and he may have included in that claim something peculiarly his own. He had seen the look in Christ's eyes when his voice of denial was loud in the courtyard. He remembered too how he and two others had seen the glory of the Lord—a Shekinah indeed, again to be revealed. And above all he remembered the injunction which is the core and center of his appeal.

Peter had walked with the Lord on the stony beach on the northwest shore of Galilee, where the

Church of Peter's Secrecy stands today. Perhaps the sun, coming up over the Golan Heights, was turning the lake to a sheet of silver with the Heights dark mauve beneath. There he had been recommissioned and forgiven. Thirty years later John was to tell all he could of that story, in the last chapter of his Gospel, which he had never intended to write. Could there be stronger confirmation of Peter's authorship than these almost unconscious echoes of experience woven into his language? There is more to come, but let us in the meantime linger over the thought that the apostle seeks to pass on. The shepherd's task is real and, like the elder's duty, demands the very best of man. No task, in fact, within the borders of God's service, asks or deserves anything less than the whole vitality of the committed life.

The function of the elder is pastoral (v. 2). He is the shepherd of the flock of God with all that which the name, in an Eastern context, implies (John 10 and 21:19). The figure of speech runs right through the Bible and is applied indifferently to God himself (Ps. 23) and to those who guide in his name (1 Cor. 9:7). The archetype is Moses, the petulant and imperious prince of Egypt, who was sent into the wilderness to learn shepherding, and with that calling to acquire the quiet patience and forbearance with the stupid and the weak which any ruler of men must acquire or fail in his task and purpose.

The quality of the shepherd is selfless concern for

his sheep (v. 3). He who commercializes the affairs of the spirit, seeks material advantage in the offices of the Church (Acts 8:20), or who regards eminence in the congregation as an occasion for self-exaltation and the petty enjoyment of authority, degrades a noble vocation of spiritual leadership, drains it of all real significance, and soils its glory.

Those interested in this imagery could pursue it into John Milton's *Lycidas* and John Ruskin's penetrating comments on that fine poem in *Sesame and Lilies*, Lecture One. There is a powerful passage in *Lycidas* (lines 114–29) about the false pastors against whom Peter has directed his words of warning.

Enow of such as for their bellies' sake
Creep, and intrude, and climb into the fold?
Of other care they little reckoning make,
Than how to scramble at the shearers' feast,
And shove away the worthy bidden guest;
Blind mouths! that scarce themselves know how to hold
A sheep-hook, or have learn'd aught else the least
That to the faithful herdman's art belongs!
What recks it them? What need they? They are sped;
And when they list, their lean and flashy songs
Grate on their scrannel pipes of wretched straw;
The hungry sheep look up, and are not fed,
But, swoln with wind, and the rank mist they draw,
Rot inwardly, and foul contagion spread:
Besides what the grim wolf with privy paw
Daily devours apace, and nothing said. . . .

In the same way, I appeal to you younger men to show deference to the elders. Gird yourselves with humility because God stands against the proud and gives grace to the humble (5:5).

Young and old have their duties. A becoming respect for older men is enjoined upon the younger, but such relationships, like those of wife and husband, fall smoothly into place and lose all awkwardness and tension when the overruling power of Christian love reigns in a group or section of society. Young and old both fall so far short of God who rules and governs both that differences between man and man—be it differences of years, of wealth, or ability, or any other of those measures of petty worth which man applies to man—fall away before the thought of a common allegiance to one Lord and Master.

The word translated "gird yourselves" is an interesting one—*engkomboomai*. The word *kombos* in Greek means a band, a tape, a girth, anything used to tie something round the waist. Peter bade his readers in 1:13 to "gird up the loins of your mind" (KJV), and there he used a different verb, one closely related to the verb used by John when he described Peter's tying the skirts of his cloak round his waist before splashing ashore to meet Christ (John 21:7). Now he uses the word connected with *kombos*. An *engkomboma* was an apron, something tied around the waist. And that, in a scene Peter could never forget, was what Christ wore when he washed the disciples' feet and when Peter uttered two passionate and impulsive sentences (John 13:4–8). Was there ever such an illustration of humility? And again what a touch of truth. The word for "proud" is a repulsive one in Greek, an expression filled with arrogance, haughtiness, disdain, contempt—everything which goes to make "the proud glory of life," and construct the most ungodly of characters.

> Bow down then under God's strong hand, that in his own good time he may lift you, casting all your care upon him because he does care for you. Discipline yourselves and keep alert, for your adversary, the devil, prowls around like a roaring lion looking for someone to swallow up. Resist him, solid in your faith, knowing that the brotherhood in all the world pays the same tax of suffering. And the God of all grace, who called you and who, in Christ, invited you to share his everlasting glory, after your brief suffering, will make you whole, will strengthen you, make you steadfast and set you on a firm foundation. And to him be power for ever. Amen (5:6–11).

Therefore, Peter concludes, remembering again what has haunted his mind through the whole letter—that tomorrow remained for them to face, and tomorrow was dark and menacing—therefore cast yourselves on God. The "shadow of a great right hand" of Thackeray's phrase is over all. Roll your burdens on him. The thought is an echo of Psalm 55:12, and Matthew 6:25–31.

"Be calm and watchful," he continues (v. 8, Goodspeed). Matthew 24:42 is in Peter's mind. Calmness and awareness are necessary, for there is a mind behind evil, an intelligence which plots temptation. Who can doubt it who has been at all aware of the fierce resistance to good, the unending battle, the plotted, clever ambush along life's path? Such a lot is common to man (v. 9), an important truth for the tested and the assailed to master. Others are similarly beleaguered. There is nothing unique, nothing sinful in temptation. Sin begins where resistance ceases and where the enemy wins surrender or welcome. "Withstand, rocklike in your faith," the command runs (v. 9), "knowing that the brotherhood in all the world pays the same tax of suffering." This version underlines the two inbuilt metaphors. They are strong words which tell of what God will do.

Over against all plotting evil stands the invincible God, replete with all resources (v. 10). The verse contains another interesting metaphor. The word translated "make you whole" ("perfect" in KJV) is related to the word used of James and John who were "mending" their nets in their boat at the time when the writer of the letter and his brother were called to be fishers of men (Mark 1:19). Damaged in our calling or in the useful service of our God, our nets, torn and frayed in our fishing, the skillful hands of the Master will restore, repair and strengthen. The benediction follows (v. 11).

POSTSCRIPT

By the hand of Silvanus, whom I account your faithful brother, I have written this short letter, encouraging you and telling you sincerely that this grace in which you stand is truly the grace of God. She that is in Babylon, chosen like you, sends greeting. So does Mark, my son. Greet one another with a kiss of love. Peace to all of you who are Christ's (5:12-14).

The letter ends, as do hundreds of surviving letters from the ancient world, with personal details and greetings. Peter took the pen and concluded. Paul did likewise when he wrote to the Galatians (6:11-18), apologizing for his large letters. He was probably suffering from the migrainelike effects of the Asiatic malaria which was probably his "thorn in the flesh" (2 Cor. 12:7).

Silvanus, who wrote the letter, probably carried it around the churches. As the one-time companion of Paul and Timothy, Silvanus (Silas for short) knew much of the area to which the letter was sent. This, indeed, might explain a few obscurities. Knowing Peter's intention, he could explain.

Babylon was Rome (Rev. 14:8, 16:19, 18:2). It can hardly have been what was left of the old oppressor on the Euphrates, and in this time of growing tension the Church was using a coded, cryptic language, seen in full flower in the Apocalypse.

Mark was with Peter as he was later to be with Paul (2 Tim. 4:11). He was Peter's spiritual son and companion. A teenage boy at the time of Christ's death, the son of Mary in whose "upper room" the "last supper" was eaten, Mark was probably the young man who, having followed the group in anxious curiosity to Gethsemane with a sheet hastily pulled from his bed around him, was almost arrested with the Lord (Mark 14:51, 52). It was a sudden impulse which inspired the lad. He watches under the olive trees, sure that some crisis is at hand. A flare of torches, and the betrayer is there. With a boy's reckless loyalty he shouts some protest, and angry hands lay hold of him. Slipping out of his sheet, Mark escapes. Perhaps he bore a cruel and mutilating swordslash across his fingers, for an old tradition says that in the Early Church Mark was called "the Stumpfingered."

Shall imagination be followed a little further? Did the savage blow and the cry of his young friend stir Peter to draw his long fisherman's blade and slash back at the offender?

We next meet Mark perhaps fifteen years later, a missionary, and disastrously unsuccessful. With Paul and Barnabas, John Mark has reached Perga, a port of Asia Minor. Suddenly, and for no reason stated in the text, Mark leaves the party. Mark's reason must have angered and disappointed Paul, for some years later, when Barnabas sought to include his relative for a second missionary journey, a "sharp contention" rose between him and Paul, and the two great men parted.

Perhaps Mark was a narrow nationalist, unable to share Paul's vision of the empire for Christ. Peter had found the same bold concept difficult. He was the very one to nurse the hurt, bewildered young man back to life and vigor. He set him to work writing the Gospel, which, in the ancient world, was sometimes called "the Gospel of Peter."

The "kiss of love" is not a direction applicable in other contexts of time and place. Phillips boldly renders: "Give one another a hearty handshake all round as a sign of love." To be sure, Paul had given the same direction (Rom. 16:16; 1 Cor. 16:20; 2 Cor. 13:12; 1 Thess. 5:26).

At the same time, even in the ancient world, the practice was embarrassing. Clement of Alexandria, writing late in the second century, said: "Love is not judged by a kiss but by goodwill. Some do nothing but fill the churches with the noise of kissing. . . . And there is an impure kiss full rather of poison than of holiness." It was a custom which was regulated, confined to men, and gradually dwindled. Scripture must be applied to alien situations with discernment.

*   *   *

And so we say farewell to Peter. He is a strong and active figure right from the day when we first meet him—called to follow Christ and fish for men—on to the centurion's house in the garrison town by the sea. A generation later he is far from Caesarea, in the capital of the empire, the center of the threatening menace of that perilous decade. He has said much which we too should hear in a world where the same darkness haunts corners of tyranny, a world not without the creeping shadows of the dark. Tomorrow is veiled. Evil still strives hard against the good. The lion still roars. The faith they held in Asia and in Rome still stands. Multitudes still hold it, as did our loved ancestors in the Church, as a treasure more precious than life. And let us face tomorrow, whatever tomorrow be, in its strength.

And now, heads bowed, we hear Peter's benediction: "Peace be with you all who are in Jesus Christ." Amen.